The Life of the Harp Seal

The Life of the Harp Seal

photography and text by Fred Bruemmer

Times BOOKS

New York

Editorial and graphic contributors:

Design: Gerald M. Muir
Editors: Paul Rush, Anna Ozvoldik
Cartography: The Graphic Group
Special Holloway Photography: Courtesy of Newfoundland Archives
Special Underwater Photography: Courtesy of Dr. Joseph B. MacInnis
Produced under the direction of: Optimum Publishing Company Limited

Published in the United States by Times Books,
a division of Quadrangle/The New York Times Book Company, Inc.

For information address:
Times Books,
Quadrangle/The New York Times Book Co., Inc.
Three Park Avenue,
New York, N.Y. 10016

Published simultaneously in Canada by Optimum Publishing Company Limited,
Montreal.

Library of Congress Cataloging in Publication Data

Bruemmer, Fred

   The life of the harp seal.
   1. Harp seal 2. Sealing 1. Title
QL737. P64B78 1977   599.748   77-79023
ISBN O-8129-0707-8

Preface

Thirteen years ago, in December of 1964, I flew to the small, isolated village of La Tabatière on the north shore of the Gulf of St. Lawrence. One hundred and thirty-one years earlier, in the summer of 1833, the famous painter-naturalist John James Audubon had stopped at this spot "To visit ... the Seal establishment of a Scotchman, Samuel Robertson ..." I lived with Samuel Robertson's great-great-grandson, Ronald Robertson, who, with other members of La Tabatière's Robertson clan, pursues the "seal fishery," the capture of migrating harp seals, much as his ancestors have done for the past 170 years.

In March of 1965, I travelled with a group of Canadian scientists aboard an icebreaker to the "Front," to those vast fields of pack ice off southern Labrador and northern Newfoundland that are the cradle of the seals.

Since then, I have returned to the ice in the Gulf of St. Lawrence or on the "Front" nearly every spring, with scientists, with sealers, with conservationists. To all of them I am deeply grateful for their help, for taking me to the ice and the seals, and for sharing with me their vast knowledge of seals and sealing.

I am particularly indebted to Dr. A.W. Mansfield, Dr. David E. Sergeant, Mr. Brian Beck, Mr. Wybrant Hoek, and Mr. G.A. Sleno of the Arctic Biological Station, Fisheries And Marine Service, Department of Fisheries And The Environment; to Mr. Stanley Dudka, Field Supervisor of International Surveillance, Department of Fisheries And The Environment; to Mr. Brian D. Davies, Executive Director of the International Fund For Animal Welfare, Inc., and to Mr. Hanns Ebensten and Mr. Brian Kenny of Hanns Ebensten Travel, Inc. I am grateful to Dr. Joseph B. MacInnis for permission to use his underwater pictures of seals, and to Mr. David Davis, Archivist of the Newfoundland Provincial Archives in St. John's for making available the superb and evocative Holloway pictures of long-ago sealing. To my wife, Maud, I owe thanks for innumerable reasons, for help, and love, and understanding.

Fred Bruemmer
Montreal, 1977

Contents

Chapter one
"The Lamb Of God."

During the night the wind shifted to the northeast and increased in strength. Responding to its pressure, the vast ice masses in the Gulf of St. Lawrence begin to move. The paper-thin, new ice upon the inky-black leads, separating the immense, irregular floes, crumples with a whispering sound. It is intensely cold. The stars glitter through the clear air. The light of a three-quarter moon quicksilvers a path across the water and glints upon the splintering ice.

With the terrifying, inexorable power of millions of tons of ice set in motion, the giant floes collide. Their edges grind together, harsh and grating, the pressure increases, the ice groans and shudders, the two-foot-thick floes buckle and break. House-high chunks of ice tilt up in slow motion, topple over and crash, playthings of titanic forces.

The floes begin to rafter. They override each other; the edge of one is pushed down into the water, while the other slides above it. Water gurgles up between the floes, is soaked up avidly by the dry snow covering the ice and turns it into greyish, saline mush. The vast world of ice is in motion, the floes gyrate and shift, the crash and screech of riven ice fills the night.

Near sunrise the wind abates. The movement of the ice ceases. For a while the floes still creak against each other, heaved-up sheets of ice slip and shatter.

The floes are transformed from the previous day. Then, under a cloudy sky, they appeared like an infinite expanse of mat, egg-shell white, seamed with soot-black leads, an immense jigsaw puzzle of ice and water, of black and white. Now, where the floes have interlocked, their broken pieces rear up into pressure ridges, six-foot-high meandering hills of jumbled ice. The sun rises above the horizon. Its slanting rays strike the ice in sparks of frozen fire.

Seals lie near the edge of the floes, dark spindle shapes upon the snow. For a few weeks in late winter, the pack ice is their realm. They are harp seals; Pagophilus groenlandicus, scientists call them, 'Greenland's ice-loving' seals. They haul out onto the ice to bear their pups, here, in the Gulf of St. Lawrence; on the "Front Ice," off the east coast of southern Labrador and northern Newfoundland; on the "West Ice" east of Greenland; and on the ice of Russia's White Sea.

The harp seal's life cycle and vast annual migrations move in rhythm with the formation and disintegration of the immense northern ice fields. The pups are born in the last days of February and in March, when the ice cover reaches its maximum extent. The seals moult in April and May, as the ice begins to break up. And in summer they migrate north, following the receding ice. Some harp seals of the White Sea herd swim as far as northern Spitsbergen and Franz Josef Land, to within five hundred miles of the North Pole.

The kiss of recognition: the female harp seal identifies her pup by smell.

In a dark pool of water among the floes a seal's head bobs up. The female breathes in deeply and exhales with a snort. Glittering water droplets quiver on her droopy whiskers. She is about to give birth and must haul out onto the ice, but she hesitates. In the water she feels safe. She moves in it with seemingly effortless speed and grace. Her large, brown, slightly protuberant eyes give her better vision in the dim, pellucid green of the sea, than in the harsh glare upon the ice. Her true home is the sea, but now as she must renew the eternal cycle of life, her ancient land lineage asserts itself.

Eons ago, her ancestors roamed the land. Small, perhaps dog-like, they scavenged along river banks and coastal beaches. The rich sea beckoned. Increasingly they specialized in gathering food from its waters. Over millions of years, the infinitely patient, probing processes of evolution transformed them into animals that may have resembled otters, equally at home on land and in water. In the Oligocene, some 30 million years ago, evolutionary change tipped in favor of life in the sea. Hind feet became webbed to provide efficient propulsion in water. The body was wrapped in highly insulating blubber to protect it from the sapping chill of the sea. The animal, now a seal, became streamlined, its smooth torpedo-shape gliding through the water in fast and dexterous pursuit of fleet but abundant prey. The sea had claimed them but, unlike the whales, whose ancestors left the land more than a 100 million years ago never to return, the land retains part of its ancient hold upon the seals. To bear their young they must come back to it or to its marine equivalent, the ice.

The female exhales, twists backwards and somersaults down through the water with fluid grace. Her broad, webbed hind flippers fan out alternately to push her forward and are feathered on the backstroke. Her massive body undulates slightly in rhythm with her flipper movements. Her foreflippers are short, sharp-clawed, powerful. Over millions of years, the front legs of her land ancestors shrunk; now only the broad hand-like flippers remain, pressed tightly into slight depressions of her body, the modified armpits, so as not to interfere with the superbly streamlined shape.

She glides idly, irresolutely back and forth, just a few feet beneath the surface, torn between fear to be on the ice and the nearness and urgency of birth which impels her to haul out, despite her fears. Should there be no ice, she can, in some mysterious way, delay birth for many days. One late winter, a few years ago, there was hardly any ice in the Gulf of St. Lawrence. This female, and tens-of-thousands of others searched for it, urgently, desperately. Guided by ice-cooled layers of water, and by ice-blink, the light reflection of ice fields upon a cloudy sky, they finally found the only ice in the vastness of the Gulf. But it was weak ice, thin, broken, the snow upon it waterlogged.

Harp seals surface in a lead among the floes.

The females hauled out on it. Their pups were born and lay shivering upon the wet ice. They suckled greedily, but most were doomed. The wet snow matted their downy-soft fur, the icy wind drained heat from their bodies faster than they could generate it. Constantly cold, they whimpered and many died.

A few days later, a southwesterly gale broke up even this precarious haven, fragmented the floes and nearly all the pups who had survived until then drowned. The females who had reached the ice too late, gave birth at sea. Their pups swam for a few moments, their tiny, weak flippers moving instinctively. They squalled with fear and cold. The water paralyzed them and within a minute of birth the tiny flame of life was snuffed out by the frigid sea.

This year the ice is perfect, the floes large and strong. The female surfaces near the ice edge, and pushes herself up with rapidly sculling flippers until she rises nearly chest-high out of the water. She sees other seals on the ice and feels reassured. Intensely gregarious, she is apprehensive and restless unless other seals are nearby. She dives again, briefly, surfaces with a rush and slithers onto the ice. In the water she was a being of infinite grace and beauty, her massive-looking body amazingly flexible. On the ice she moves slowly. She digs the sharp claws of her foreflippers into the ice like crampons and hitches her 380-pound body forward in labored, ungainly humps. Once she comes too close to another seal, is attacked and flees rapidly, scrabbling over the ice in frantic haste, her hind end undulating, as if she were trying to swim. She tires quickly and rests frequently. The breeze and flying snow crystals irritate her large eyes. Like all seals, she lacks nasolachrymal ducts that carry excess tear fluid from the eyes to the nasal passage. (That is why, when we cry, we sniffle.) Tears splash down her face and mat the fur beneath her eyes. She looks sad and worried.

Cradle of the harp seals: the ice floes in the Gulf of St. Lawrence.

Above left:
As a strange pup approaches her, the
female seal rears up in threat posture.

Above right:
Harp seal mother suckling her pup.

After a brief, identifying glance, the other seals ignore her as long as she does not approach too close. Gregarious as the harp seals are, on the ice each female has her individual distance, a private territory she defends against all the other seals, even against other pups. The female lies down near an ice hummock then, restless, moves on. She passes too near another seal; it rears up on its front flippers, twists its head backwards and warns her with a gurgling, high-pitched, threatening trill.

The female humps aside, her trail a trough of compacted snow flanked by the hook marks of her front flippers. Finally she finds a place she likes: from it she can see the other seals but is far enough from them to avoid conflicts. She breathes deeply; her dark, v-shaped nostril slits open and close with spasmic abruptness. She moans heavily, her body twists. Suddenly she lifts her abdomen, her hind flippers, usually pressed together, like hands in prayer, flare and with one tremendous muscular contraction she expels the pup from her body.

It lies on the ice, quite still, wrapped in its moist, glistening caul, a small, steaming parcel of life, delivered with shocking abruptness from the cozy, dark womb of its mother, with its steady, humid, tropical climate of 98° F, into the icy, blinding glare of a new world. With an abrupt twist of her hind quarters, the mother snaps the umbilical cord. The link of common life is severed, the little pup is a new and separate being. Wailing, a flock of herring gulls wheels down and settles on the ice, waiting to eat the afterbirth.

The female ignores them. In orderly sequence she repeats the movements other female harp seals have made at the time of birth for millennia. She turns and nuzzles her pup, breaks the thin fetal membrane that envelops it and licks it matted fur. She inhales deeply, repeatedly, and the distinctive odor of her pup becomes fixed in her mind. From this moment on, for the next three weeks, she will know her pup by its smell from all the other, apparently identical, harp seal pups born on the ice. This infinitesimal variation in smell which distinguishes her pup from all the hundreds of thousands of others, triggers and determines her response to it. She will nurse it and protect it, she may face death to shield it, but she will repel any other pup that comes near her.

The pup stirs. It blinks its large, dark, lustrous eyes. It flexes its limp little hind flippers that were tightly furled, like leaves in a bud, within the confines of the amnion. It mews feebly and inhales. Its long fur is still moist, and tinted yellowish by the amniotic fluid. Its big-headed, spindly body is lean, as yet no protective blubber covers it. Cold penetrates its fur and the pup shivers violently. Its cries become louder, more desperate; the plaintive wails are carried by the wind over the immensity of the ice. Like its smell, the timbre and pattern of its voice become imprinted upon its mother's mind for a period of three weeks and are then erased forever. During this time, in the shifting, drifting world of the ice pack, alive with the bleats of tens of thousands of seal pups, she will be able to recognize, by variations far too fine to be distinguished by the human ear, the call of her pup amongst those of all the others.

Hooded seals, too, give birth to their slate-blue pups on the ice of the Gulf of St. Lawrence.

Indistinctly, the pup sees nearby a large, dark shape upon the glaring white. Slowly it creeps towards it. Its hunger, the urgent, vital need for food, and the warmth and smell of its mother's body excite the little pup. It must nurse, that it knows, but it does not know where.

Responding to her pup's frantic cries and the prodding of its little muzzle, the female turns onto her side. The pup snuffles hopefully along her chin and chest, sucks desperately and noisily near her flipper. The female lies quietly, patiently. The pup continues to nuzzle eagerly, nearly at random, along its mother's six-foot length, in a desperate search for the life-giving milk it knows is somewhere hidden along this warm, enticing body. It tries again near the chest, but this time the female intervenes. She waves her front flipper rapidly, its movement and a slap with the hard claws, shoo the pup further down toward the lower abdomen, the only region where its search can be successful. After fifteen minutes of increasingly frantic nuzzling, the female's flailing flipper, the slight increase in her skin temperature near the nipples and their faint but distinctive smell finally guide the pup to the right spot.

The pup sucks and the inch-long, pencil-thin nipple emerges from the skin fold beneath the fur in which it normally lies hidden. The pup suckles greedily, its eyes closed in blissful concentration. A few drops of yellowish milk trickle from the corners of its mouth. It finds the second nipple and butts the female with its muzzle. The rich, viscous milk fills its belly, warmth spreads through its body. The milk is very nutritive; it contains 42 per cent fat and 10 per cent protein, as compared to 3.4 per cent fat and 3.3 per cent protein in cow's milk. It has the consistency of thick, smooth cream.

On right:
Woolly coat and rapidly-expanding
blubber layer keep pup warm.

The ice is a precarious cradle. Storms can break it, warmth can melt it, winds and currents can scatter the floes. The longer the pups spend on the floes, the greater the dangers to which they are exposed. To shorten this dependence upon the ice, the pups must grow fast. They sleep and nurse; they expend a minimum of energy and try to absorb a maximum amount of food.

As the pups swell, their mothers turn svelte. When they humped onto the ice to give birth, they were enormously fat, their whole body, with the exception of head and flippers, encased in a layer of blubber nearly two inches thick and weighing 140 pounds, more than a third of their entire weight. In the crucible of her body, the female's blubber is converted into fat-rich milk. Absorbed by the pup, the milk is reconverted into blubber. At birth, the pups are lean with only a few millimeters of fat beneath the skin that hangs in loose folds, like a fur coat many sizes too large. In five days this film of fat expands into a blubber layer an inch thick; in a fortnight it measures nearly two inches. In three weeks they will have nearly doubled their girth and more than tripled their birth weight. The blubber protects the pup from the cold of ice, and air, and sea. It also is its energy reserve, its mother's legacy to help it survive the difficult, crucial weeks after their separation.

The little pup has finished its first meal. It is replete, content, and sleepy. It yawns, stretches its flippers and looks wonderingly at the world of ice and snow around it. It dips its nose into powdery snow and its jet-black muzzle twinkles for a moment with glittering crystals. It inhales, sneezes in surprise, and learns not to lie with its nose in soft snow. The lids droop over its eyes, the pup curls up a bit, hugs itself with its short flippers and falls asleep.

A remote but steady and pervading drone fills the air. The female, sleeping beside her pup, awakes and stirs uneasily. The noise is too far to panic her, but its alien hum fills her with a vague fear. She humps a few yards across the ice, hesitates, returns, nuzzles her pup and, as if reassured by its presence, lies quietly

and goes to sleep again. High in the deep-blue sky, the plane flies in a systematic grid pattern above the seals widely scattered upon the floes. A motor-driven aerial camera clicks away methodically, producing a steady sequence of pictures whose edges slightly overlap each other.

The pictures, the biologists hope, will enable them to answer with a fair degree of accuracy the question they are asked each year: "How many harp seals are there in the Gulf?" Similar aerial photographic censuses are carried out above the seals on the "Front Ice," off Labrador and Newfoundland. Basing its decision in part on the biologists' reports, the government will decide how many seals may be killed each year.

The biologists think of the seals in terms of "game management." Their principal goal, the Holy Grail of game management, is to determine M.S.Y., maximum sustained yield, the largest number of seals that can be killed without reducing, over the long range, the total harp seal population. Their recommendations to the government evolve out of an analysis of extremely complex variables: natural mortality in harp seals (probably small in normal years; catastrophically high in years when ice is missing or unsuitable); age composition of the harp seal herds, and apparently changing patterns in the age of sexual maturity in harp seals (since their number decreased in recent decades, females seem to reach sexual maturity one or two years earlier than when populations were larger). Taking these and many other factors into account, biologists design intricate population models, devise mathematical formulae of staggering complexity which, they hope, will help them predict with precision the number of seals available for "harvesting" each year, while maintaining, at the same time, harp seal populations at their present level. In theory these are the figures that determine government-set quotas. In practice, the government is guided as much by political as by scientific considerations, for it is under considerable pressure from forces embracing totally opposed views and goals: those of the sealers and the sealing industry who, having grudgingly accepted the idea of quotas, want them maintained at the highest possible level, and those of the conservationists, who regard the killing of the seals as brutal and barbaric and who want to halt the hunt.

The little pup dreams. It moves in its sleep, its black whiskers quiver, the flippers twitch, it shivers from time to time. Its fur is dry now and begins to fluff out. Near the skin, the fine wool is tight and curly; a second coat of longer, stiffer hairs covers the dense layer of wool. Down-soft and, in a day or two, glistening white, this delicate, lustrous lanugo, or natal wool, keeps the pup warm during the first two weeks of its life until its blubber insulation is sufficiently thick to protect it from freezing wind and the chill of the sea. The white hairs are nearly transparent. The sun's rays shine through them and warm the pup's skin, and the gossamer-fine wool retains the warm air layer next to its body. Another female, about to give birth, approaches too close. The pup's mother rears up in angry protest, and snarls, shrill and threatening. The pup awakes with a start, looks around vague and incomprehending, sees the dark shapes upon the glittering snow, inhales its mother's smell and, reassured, falls asleep again.

In 1909 Dr. Wilfred T. Grenfell, the famous medical missionary to Labrador, wrote: "It has not been easy to convey to the Eskimo mind the meaning of the Oriental similies of the Bible. Thus the Lamb of God had to be translated kotik or young seal. This animal, with its perfect whiteness as it lies in its cradle of ice, its gentle, helpless nature, and its pathetic innocent eyes, is probably as apt a substitute, however, as nature offers."

Mother and pup lie on the raftered ice.
Their only enemy here is man.

Chapter two
The Place Of Birth.

Emportés par la glace, Disparus en mer, (carried away by the ice, lost at sea). The phrases run like a grim refrain through the annals of the Magdalens, those lovely islands of red sandstone, white gypsum and miles of yellow dunes and beaches spread over the sea in squiggles and blobs like writing on a birth-day cake. The sea fed the islanders; often it killed them. But the spell of the sea keeps its hold upon the people. The homes of the 14,000 Madelinots are scat-tered over the seven inhabited islands. One thing near-ly all have in common: they are built within sight of the sea.

Jacques Cartier discovered the islands in the sum-mer of 1534. On June 26 he saw the Bird Rocks. There were three islands then "as completely covered with birds... as a field is covered with grass... We killed more than a thousand... and took as many as we wished in our long-boats." The English captain Charles Leigh who passed the Bird Rocks fifty years later,

wrote: "The birds sit there as thicke as stones lie on a paved street," and when John James Audubon visited them on June 14, 1833, he "thought them covered with snow... They were birds... a mass of birds of such a size as I never before cast my eye on." Fishermen, Audubon reported, killed the birds to use them as cod bait, each boat crew of six clubbing birds at the rate of 500 an hour. Pounding waves and grinding ice have destroyed one of the islands; the second rises like a broken, jagged tooth above the water, its top covered with gannets, and only the tall, massive Bird Rock is still as Cartier saw it.

Well provisioned with salted-down birds, Cartier sailed on and came to the next island which he named Ile Brion, after his principal supporter, Philippe Chabot, seigneur de Brion, and grand admiral of France. Cartier, the usually curt and matter-of-fact mariner, was enchanted by this island and spoke of it with poetic pleasure: "One arpent of it is worth more than the whole of Newfoundland," and later he wrote to his king, François-premier; "[it] is a veritable Paradise... thick groves of splendid trees alternated with beautiful glades and meadowland, while the en-tire length of the island, about six miles, was carpeted with bright flowers, blossoming peas and the soft colors of the wild rose."

A century after Cartier, the pragmatic Samuel de Champlain, in a sort of promotional prospectus, skip-ped the blooming peas and the gentle roses, and concentrated instead on the region's sea mammal wealth. There are near these islands, he reported, vast numbers of walruses "whose tusks are better than elephant's teeth, the pound being worth 20 sols, [and there is] an abundance of seals."

Above:
On the ice near the Magdalen Islands, a female hooded seal snarls to warn an intruder away from her newborn pup.

On right:
A female harp seal surfaces among the ice floes to look for her pup.

Gregarious, harp seals like to lie in
groups upon the ice.

Basques and Bretons were already killing the walruses on the Magdalen Islands, for their hides, their blubber, and their ivory tusks. The hides, wrote the historian Richard Hakluyt in 1600, were much in demand by the leatherdressers of London, who considered them "excellent good to make light targets [shields] against the arrows of the Savages." The blubber, Hakluyt reported, was rendered into valuable "traine oyle." The ivory tusks were sold in England "to the combe and knife makers." They could also be palmed off on the more credulous as an acceptable substitute for the miraculously potent, but prohibitively expensive horn of the mythical unicorn.

Assured a ready and rewarding market for walrus products, the islanders killed in droves the "bestes à la grande dent," the beasts with the great tooth, as Champlain had called them. It was so easy. In winter and spring, the walruses kept to the ice, drifting on it above the rich shellfish banks that surround the Magdalen Islands.

In summer, with the ice gone, the walruses came ashore on traditional hauling-out places. The islanders called these places by the ancient French word 'échoueries.' There the walruses clustered in dense, malodorous conclaves, leading a life of leisure, lolling in the sun. In 1765 the surveyor-general Samuel Holland estimated their number at more than 100,000. Forty thousand, he claimed, lay hauled out on one beach alone. His figures are probably wildly exaggerated. Nevertheless, walruses in his time were still, after two centuries of slaughter, numerous on the Magdalen Islands.

The hunters, armed with guns and lances, approached a group of sleeping walruses from downwind, rushed between the animals and the sea, and stampeded them inland, where the massive, lumbering walruses were helpless and easy to kill. Two hundred to 300 were usually killed at one time. In 1765, between June 20 and August 20, four hunts were held and 2,400 walruses were killed. Occasionally ship-based men from other parts of the Maritimes and even from the United States, attracted by this lucrative hunt, joined in the massacre of walruses on land, and harpooned those that managed to escape to sea. The last Magdalen Island walrus was killed on the Petite Echouerie beach in the summer of 1799.

Above left:
A hooded seal bull, his hood inflated,
stares at a rival upon the ice.

Above right:
Hooded seals lie on the ice in family
groups: a male and a female with her
newborn pup.

In a dark pool of water among the ice floes north-west of Brion Island, a young female harp seal surfaces and inhales deeply. Almost exactly five years ago, she was born on the ice not far from here. She has returned to the Gulf every year since, but usually remained far from the breeding floes, together with other immature seals of roughly her own age. This year, a compelling urge drew her to the vast ice fields.

She has swum far to be here, nearly six thousand miles since the preceding spring. She had spent the summer off the Greenland coast, catching fish, idling through clouds of crustaceans, swimming north, ever north with 22 companions from the Gulf. One day, near the jutting, distinctive rock north of Upernavik which 19th century whalers named "The Devil's Thumb," they came upon an immense shoal of polar cod. Excited by the mass of prey, the seals rushed through the scattering fish, enveloped in a swirl of motion and glitter, and snapped up fish after fish in swift pursuit.

That night, a storm screamed across Baffin Bay. The waves rose and tumbled and churned, gale-force winds ripped off the wave crests, and spumes of angry spindrift hissed across the sea. In the turmoil of the sea, the young female lost contact with her companions. No longer did she hear the reassuring sounds of their grunting and squealing. When the storm eased, she was alone. Highly gregarious, she missed the presence of the other seals intensely. She was restless and depressed. She swam more and hunted less, seeking other seals in the vastness of the sea. After a week, she heard the familiar calls of harp seals and rushed joyfully to join them. The group consisted of animals older than she, and all were members of the Front herd; they had been born on the ice off Labrador and Newfoundland. Slightly hostile at first, suspicious of a newcomer, they chased the young female and snapped at her flippers. But soon they became used to her presence and she travelled with them for the rest of summer and fall.

Treading water, a female harp seal pushes herself high to look over the rim of the ice.

Above:
Harp seal mothers surface in glittering water.

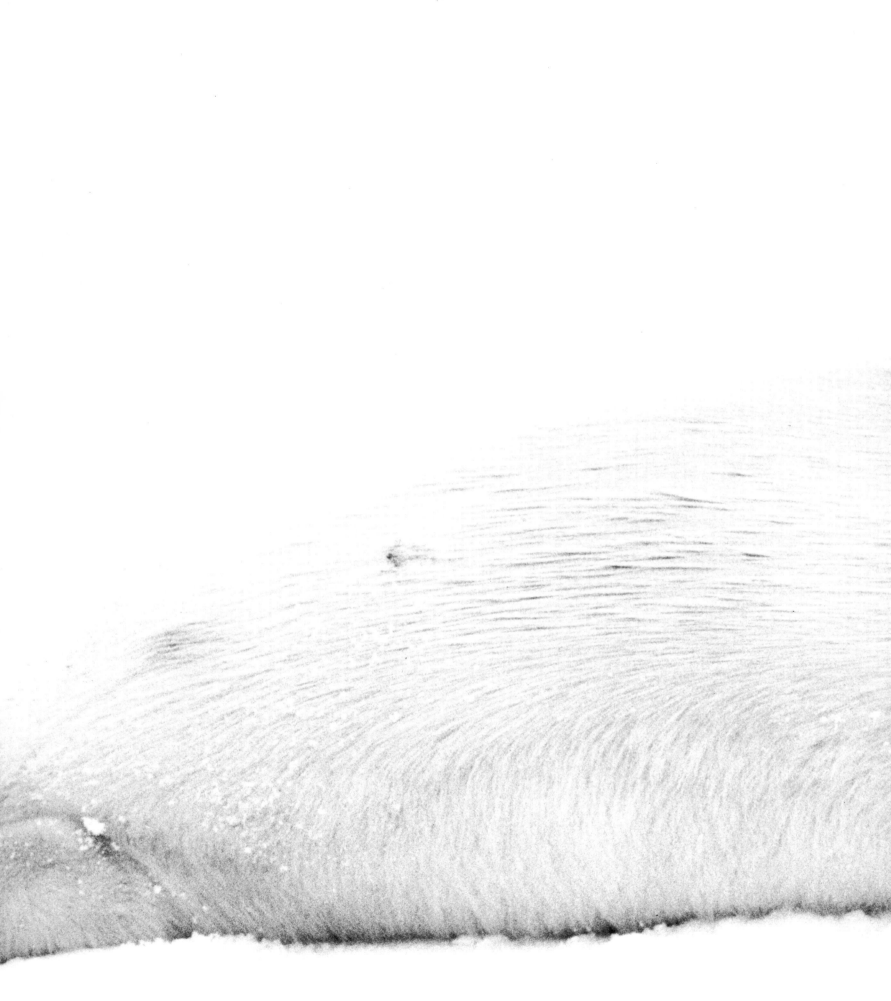

Fur-covered and well-fed, this baby seal looks like a child's bedtime toy.

In early October they crossed Davis Strait and then swam leisurely southward with the Labrador Current, gorging on the abundant capelin, diving deep occasionally to rip into the dull-colored, dim-witted cod. By now the female was a fully accepted member of the group. Together they hunted, together they swam south, together they raced, and jumped and porpoised, arching out of the water, blithe spirits of the sea. 'Kaerolit,' the jumping seals, Eskimos call them.

In December they reached southern Labrador, still swimming in a southeasterly direction, a few miles off the village of Battle Harbour where, according to Labrador lore, Eskimos were attacked and massacred by European fishermen and their Indian allies many centuries ago. The fight may have taken place, for European fishermen did exterminate Eskimos all along the south Labrador coast, but Battle Harbour owes its name to the milder pursuits. It is a corruption of the Portuguese 'batal,' boat, and originally just meant 'Boat Harbour.'

The seals were following the Labrador Current, its icy waters carrying them leisurely south and east. Her companions were content, but the young female was restless again, for here an imperative demand urged her to change course and swim west. Many subtle factors added up to stir this compulsion within her: the changing shape of the distant, dimly seen but vaguely remembered coast; slight variations in water temperature; infinitely minute changes in the very taste and texture of the sea, produced by local currents. Sensitive nerves relayed these messages to the brain which, in some unkown way, compared them to impulses received in previous years, and perhaps even held stored within itself the memory not only of this seal but that of thousands upon thousands of her ancestors born in the Gulf. The messages triggered in the mind of the young female the powerful urge to swim west.

On right:
A harp seal pup lies near the shimmering
ice blocks of a pressure ridge.

She felt tense and distraught, torn by the stress of conflicting drives and desires. She was happy with the seals she had joined and with whom she had travelled for so many months. Their voices in the sea reassured her, their nearness comforted her. Like all gregarious animals, she felt a passionate need to stay with the group. But their way was not her way, they were called towards regions different from the one that was now calling her with such imperious force.

Irresolute, she left the group then, in a rush of sudden fear, rejoined them. But finally the call of the Gulf, of her natal place, was stronger than her dread of being alone. She left the others, struck out towards the west and passed through the Strait of Belle Isle into the Gulf of St. Lawrence. There she had fallen in with other seals of the Gulf herd, but in late February another urgent summons permeated her body and forced her to swim south and seek out the great ice fields where she had been born five years ago.

Sculling rapidly with her hind flippers, the young female rises high out of the water to look over the ice rim that surrounds the pool. Concentric ripples spread outward from her slightly swaying body and ruffle the satin-smooth surface of the water. She spots dark shapes upon the floes near the water's edge, turns onto her back and crosses the pool with leisurely strokes, her nose rising above the water like a small periscope. She dives, loops smoothly under water, her outstretched front flippers acting as ailerons, pushes powerfully with her hind flippers, rushes upwards and the momentum carries her onto the ice. She hitches herself forward a few yards, pauses, and rears up on her front flippers for a better look around. She sees the dark shapes of other females upon the ice and, near them, their pups, slightly fuzzy forms against a backdrop of glaring white. The miracle is that she can distinguish them at all.

Above left:
The pup cries and its mother surfaces in
a nearby bobbing hole.

Above right:
When man approaches, a newborn harp
seal is both apprehensive and curious.

Millions of years ago, when her ancestors changed from land animals into creatures of the sea, their eyes had to become modified to enable them to catch fast, elusive prey deep in the oceans. The eyes became large and incredibly light-sensitive, giving the seal perfect emmetropic vision in water. An unfortunate corollary of such a design, perfect in one medium, the sea, is that it should render them nearly useless in air, their acuity curtailed by severe myopia and astigmatism: instead of being neatly focused upon the retina, light rays arrive scattered and the image should be vague, blurred and distorted. But the instant the female surfaces from the darkness of the sea into the ice-glittering glare above it, powerful sphincters, circular muscle bands, contract the pupils of her eyes, leaving open only hair-thin vertical slits. This produces the same pinhole effect a photographer achieves by closing the diaphragm of his camera down to the smallest possible f-stop: it excludes most of the scattered, incident rays, admitting only enough to form reasonably sharp images upon an exceedingly light-sensitive retina, and thus the seal, whose eyes are so superbly designed for vision in the low-light conditions of the dark sea, achieves the seemingly impossible: it also sees well, albeit slightly shortsightedly and a bit diffuse, when upon the ice.

A slight breeze drifts across the ice and carries with it the voices of the seals: the tremulous cry of a newborn pup; the snarl of an annoyed female; the gurgling treble trill uttered as warning; the wail of a hungry pup. The young female inhales deeply, her dark nostrils flare and close abruptly. Her brain absorbs and decodes the myriad messages of smell and sound and sight, but none here elicit a response to her restless quest dictated by changes within her body.

On right:
Among the whiteness of the snow, a
white harp seal pup: two large, dark eyes,
a black muzzle and dark droopy
whiskers.

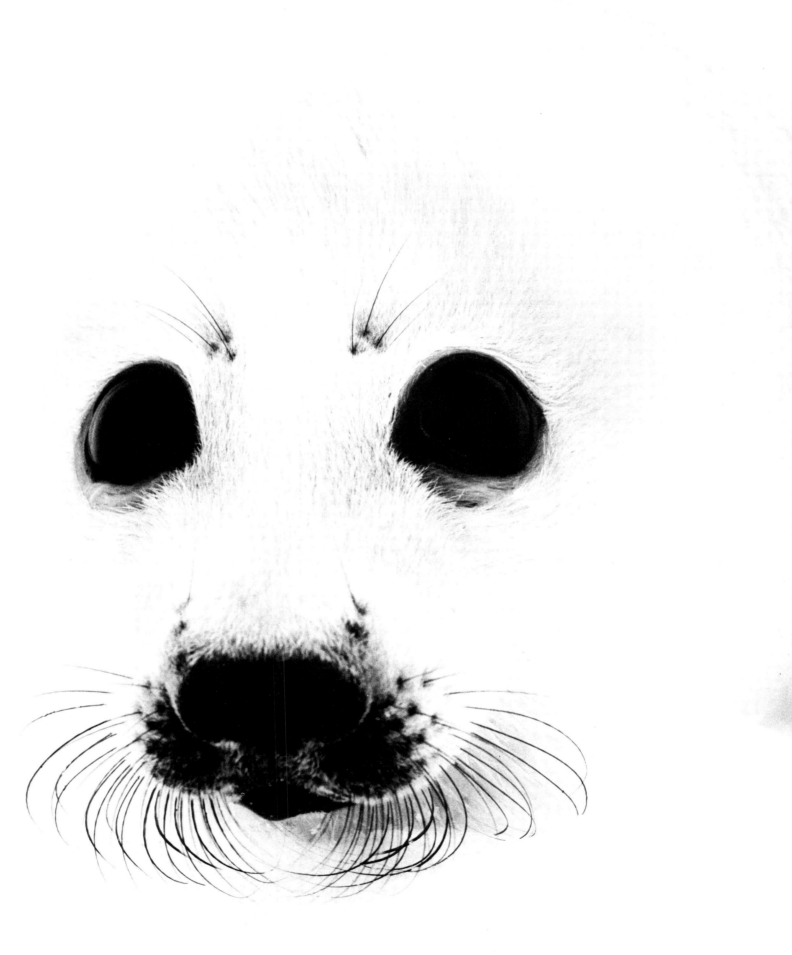

She sinks down upon the ice, her pliable rib cage bends outward under her weight and she becomes oddly flat, like a half-deflated tire. She digs the claws of her front flippers into the ice and slowly pulls herself back towards the open water. She hears a far-away, harsh and rhythmic throb, gaining quickly in intensity as the helicopter comes nearer. Half alarmed, half curious, she stops. The helicopter lands at some distance, churning up billows of snow. A guide quickly climbs out from his seat next to the pilot. Three well-muffled tourists, packed in the rear, manage to open the doors, disentangle themselves and their cameras, climb out warily, duck apprehensively under the whirling rotor and assemble in a little worried cluster next to their guide. The helicopter lifts with a metallic roar, swoops across the ice, gains altitude and vanishes landwards to pick up the next load of tourists. After the racket, it suddenly seems very quiet. A vast stillness lies over the ice, broken only by the protesting barks and snarls of the upset seals a few hundred yards away. The guide, a veteran sealer, walks across the ice with the assurance of experience, and the tourists follow obediently in his tracks.

The young female, frightened by the helicopter, flees towards the water, scrabbling and undulating across the ice. Most of the other females remain, the bond binding them to their pups stronger than their fear of the distant noise. The young female reaches the edge of the pool and slides into it with one smooth motion. She still hears the noise in the water, but now she feels secure. She dives and glides softly, smoothly through the greenish, diaphanous depth beneath the floes. Here and there through gaps in the ice, the sun pours down into the sea, like shafts of light through high cathedral windows.

Gaining speed and momentum under water, a harp seal female rushes up onto the ice.

From left to right:
The baby harp seal nudges its mother so
she will turn onto her side and let it nurse.

The pup sucks hopefully, but in the wrong place.

Harp seal mother nursing her pup.

*Happy and replete after the meal, the
seal pup plays with its flipper.*

Chapter three
Of Seals And Man

In January and February, as the ice fields grew on the Gulf of St. Lawrence, many of the pregnant harp seals sought out the regions with the strongest floes. They scraped holes through the ice with their powerful, long-clawed foreflippers and kept them open by surfacing frequently in them and by scratching away new-formed ice. Each time they surfaced, a bit of water sloshed over the edge of these "bobbing holes," as Newfoundland sealers call them. Eventually most holes were surrounded by low, glistening cones of ice.

In the shifting world of wind-driven, current-carried ice, these bobbing holes became for many females the focal point of a mobile home territory. When their time arrived, they hauled out through these holes and bore their pups near them on the ice. Other females chose the edges of leads and open pools among the floes, but when winds and currents closed them, their escape route into the sea was blocked.

As the tourists and their guides approach, the female seals react to powerful, conflicting impulses. Fear of man, their most recent and most deadly enemy, urges them to flee and seek safety in the sea; the strong bond of maternal love that binds them to their pups, constrains them to stay. They hump hurriedly towards their holes, pause, and return to their pups. As the people come nearer, fear, in most seals, outweighs affection. They scramble rapidly across the ice and slip into the water. They surface moments later, and look towards their pups with bulging, worried eyes.

One female lies with her pup near a pressure ridge. The day before a lead of open water separated her floe from the one next to it. The strong wind of the preceding night has driven the floes together. The female searches frantically for an escape hole. There is an opening, but it is filled with ice ground into mush by the grating floes. She forces her head down through the tightly packed ice chips and flings her body high to achieve straight downward pressure. Her hind end and rear flippers waggle frantically in the air. Finally her weight squeezes the body through the midriff bulge, she slides into the sea, and the ice closes above her.

Above left:
A harp seal pup searches for its mother.

Above right:
A pup nurses avidly; the time from birth to weaning is short.

A female surfaces near a pup. Its mother is set to repel her.

A few females remain with their pups. As the tourists come near, they rush a few yards towards them and snarl and trill their warning, then turn and hump back to the pups. In one young mother who, during the previous night has given birth to her first pup, the drive to flee and the desire to stay are nearly evenly matched. Unable to decide, she rushes back and forth between the water and her pup then, suddenly, in a fit of frustration and redirected aggression, she gives her pup a clout with her flipper that sends it tumbling across the ice.

Two helicopters shuttle back and forth between a motel on the Magdalens and the ice west of Brion Island, bringing more visitors to see the seals. They have travelled far to be here: some are from California, Arkansas, New Mexico. Most are city people. They live in a world made by man, a world of concrete and glass and steel, and while it provides them with comfort, it also creates a sense of remoteness and alienation from the land, from nature, from animals. Although it does not really affect their lives they feel, deep within, a sharp sense of loss and regret each time they read that another tract of wilderness has been erased, that yet another animal species is about to vanish forever. They feel a need to have some contact, however brief and tenuous, with a world that is not of man but of nature. So when a travel agency advertised tours to the remote and vaguely romantic ice in the Gulf of St. Lawrence to see the seals, they signed up and now they are here.

Their thrill of expectation and adventure was for a while considerably dampened by the realities of weather and ice. First a storm made flying impossible. Then the pilots could not find the seal herds. They had last been reported on the ice nearly due west of the Magdalen Islands. But the wind had shifted the floes and another day was lost while one of the helicopters criss-crossed the ice looking for the main seal concentrations where as many as 5,000 harp seals lie hauled out on each square mile of ice. The pilot spotted them late in the afternoon, dark dots on a vast expanse of white.

This day the weather is perfect and the tourists are enchanted. The sun is dazzling upon the ice, the air as clear and heady as champagne; the belligerent female seals are beautiful if somewhat frightening and the pups are utterly adorable. A few tourists coo and croon over the woolly, big-eyed little creatures; most of the pups are less delighted. Those born within the last two days are more puzzled than afraid. Not yet hungry but made vaguely uneasy by the distant noise of the helicopters and the absence of that big, dark shape near them which meant food and security, they creep a little way across the ice, whimpering petulantly. The dark shapes of people attract them; anything dark to them signifies mother and milk. At the same time they are vaguely aware that something is wrong. Mother is large, dark, nearby and horizontal. The creatures that now approach are also dark but oddly vertical and elongated. The pups stare at the tourists in wonder, confused, trusting, hopeful. A little pup, barely twelve hours old, its fluffy fur still yellowish, crawls towards a tourist kneeling on the ice to take its picture. It comes right up to him, sniffs him and backs up, startled. The smell is alien and anything strange produces fear. Crying softly, the pup crawls away again, stares once more at the strange, bad-smelling being and, tired from the exertion, falls asleep.

A female keeps a watchful eye as she surfaces in slush between floes.

Most of the older pups are apprehensive. The flight of their mothers has alarmed them. A few try to follow the females, but once the mothers have disappeared, they don't quite know where to go and move aimlessly, disconsolately across the ice, bleating plaintively. A tourist comes close. The pup tries to flee, scrambles clumsily over the ice, then, sensing the hopelessness of this action, turns and faces the ominous being with a snarl of pathetic miniature defiance, the vivid rose-pink of its mouth like a little flame in all this whiteness.

The two guides from the Magdalen Islands are worried and alert. They know from past experience that these tourists, at first so timid and obedient, are liable, once they gain courage, to disperse across the ice and may even jump blithely onto another floe without testing its strength. Patiently, politely, they try and keep their flock together; they warn, they explain, they advise. A few of the tourists who had envisioned sealers as primitive, fiendish brutes, find it hard to reconcile this mental image with these friendly, courteous men.

A tall, middle-aged lady tries to make friends with a reluctant pup. She talks to it in sweet little endearments, but the pup is not moved; the noise is strange and worries it. She takes a lot of pictures and, when the film is finished, runs back to where she left her camera bag to get a new roll. She steps onto an abandoned bobbing hole, thinly crusted by ice, hidden by drifted snow, and sinks abruptly with a cry of surprise. An ample bosom and instinctively outflung arms prevent her from sliding in entirely, and the guides extract her with some difficulty.

The pups' ambiguous behavior when faced by man, a mixture of innocence and innate fear, and their shrill, persistent bleating which widely advertises their presence, indicate that their floating nurseries are well chosen: no enemies, apart from man, threaten the pups on the ice. Once, polar bears may have killed some harp seal pups. Long ago, they ranged much further south than they do now. On May 21, 1534, when Jacques Cartier discovered Funk Island east of Newfoundland, home of the now extinct great auk, his men found there a bear "as big as a cow and as white as a swan that sprang into the sea in front of them." Sailing on towards Newfoundland, they overtook the swimming polar bear and killed it. Two centuries ago, polar bears were still common along the south Labrador coast. In 1775, Captain George Cartwright built a hunting-trading post at Sandwich Bay. In a stream nearby "salmon innumerable were leaping into the air and a grand concourse of white bears were diving after them. Others were walking along shore, and others were going in and out of the woods." He shot six in one day. But it must have been highly exceptional for a polar bear to reach the Gulf ice and they were probably equally rare on the "Front Ice" which was liable to carry them far out into the Atlantic and then melt beneath them. Ruthless hunting and warming weather have long since wiped out polar bears along the Labrador coast.

On right:
A female throws head back to warn
against coming too close.

Sleepy and content, a harp seal pup rests
near a tilted floe.

Thus even in their remote heyday, the great white bears were, at worst, a minor menace, and no other predators threatened the pups on the ice. This was essential to the harp seals' survival and accounts, in part, for their great success as a species: long ago, before men came to the ice and killed them in legion, they numbered more than ten million. The harp seals have to face many dangers during their lives, but they are never again as vulnerable as during the first two weeks of their existence, when they can neither fight nor flee with any hope of success and are thus completely at the mercy of any predator.

Born into utter helplessness, the pups, confronted by man, react to a danger they sense but do not understand. The youngest are puzzled and perturbed. Some of the older pups try valiantly but vainly to escape or to defend themselves, and a few overwhelmed by impotent fear, drop into cataplexy. Their heartbeat slows. The pup contracts, like a frightened caterpillar, and a thick wad of skin and fat rolls from the neck over its head. It lies motionless on the ice, flippers pressed to its sides, eyes wide open, like a woolly toy. A tourist pets it. The pup does not move. He rolls it gently back and forth. The pup remains inert. Overcome by dread, the pup has withdrawn into the strange twilight world of trance. "The slaughter of the innocents in Herod's day was as child's play to the massacre" of the harp seal pups, wrote Sir Wilfred Grenfell, despite his strong sympathy for the plight of the poverty-stricken Newfoundland sealers.

In mid-afternoon, fog begins to roll in from the north. The helicopters hurry back and forth to evacuate the tourists. The guides and two tourists are still on the ice when the fog oozes over them like a clammy shroud. The guides are worried. For themselves, they have little fear. Both are sealers, both have been lost in fog before. They are hardy, competent men. They know how to survive a night on the ice, but they hate to be responsible for these fancily-clad city people. Suddenly they feel resentful; these foreigners have no business being on the ice. The tourists, two young New Yorkers with a yen for the great outdoors, try hard to be jolly but deep within, initial apprehension turns into cold fear. For a while they attempt to prove their nonchalance with nervous, inane little jokes, then they fall silent and listen tensely for the throb of the helicopter.

The world of the ice has changed with stunning abruptness. Half an hour before, it spread to the horizon in sparkling clarity. Now it lies wreathed in fog, sinister and oppressive. Directionless and all-pervading the noises of the pack drift through this moist and dismal veil: the creak and groan of the floes, the shrill plaint of the pups, the harsh snarl of an angry female, the eerie wailing of the gulls, like lost souls crying.

The helicopter clatters high overhead. The guides try to call it in by radio and fail. One guide lights a flare; it explodes with a dull thud and hisses upward, trailing an arc of brilliant color through the gloom. The helicopter drops quickly, skims over the ice, spots the anxious foursome and picks them up. As they rise through the fog, it becomes lighter, shafts of prismatic rays sparkle in the moist air. Suddenly they are above it in brilliant sunshine. Twenty minutes later they are at their cozy motel. The tourists are elated. What a marvellous adventure! The guides go home gratefully. On the pack, the long-abandoned and now desperately hungry pups cry their lament. The mothers haul out, lumber across the ice, sniff their pups in what looks like a kiss of recognition, turn onto their sides and the famished pups nurse.

One female does not return. When the helicopter landed and people walked over the ice, panic flooded her mind. She rushed to the nearest hole and dived into the sea. Even there she felt fear. She swam rapidly under the ice and surfaced in a distant pool, held far away by a remote memory of shock and violent pain. The year before, when sealers moved across the ice, she had been one of the females that refused to abandon their pups. As a sealer approached, she had rushed at him, snarling. He tried to chase her away, tried to distract her and grab the pup, but each time she lunged at him, driven by desperate fear and fury. Annoyed at the delay, knowing no government inspector was near to reproach him, the sealer moved in and when she rushed at him again, he smashed his heavy club into her open mouth to "teach her," as he put it to himself. An explosion of pain filled her; half stunned she dragged herself away, her teeth shattered, her jaw broken. The sealer clubbed the pup, skinned the quivering corpse with deft strokes of his long, razor-sharp knife and moved on to the next pup.

Much later, the female had hauled out on the ice again, dazed by pain, but impelled to rejoin her pup. The ice was streaked with blood. She humped heavily to the dark little pile of meat and bones that had been her pup and sniffed it. The smell contained a message of something that had a tremendous hold upon her being, but it was vague and strange, and mixed with other messages that prompted fear. She left, but for many days the sense of loss remained. She hauled out repeatedly in the general vicinity of where her pup had been, listening, sniffing. After a week, she forgot. Her body resorbed the milk it had produced. She came into estrus and despite her wound she mated. All that had been long ago, her jaw had mended well, but the sound and smell of humans remained associated in her mind with great pain. When the tourists came, she fled far and stayed away for a long time even after the last helicopter had left.

On right:
A field of ice for its bed, a lone pup
awaits mother's return.

Her pup is desperate. It is hungry and cries. Its plight is by no means drastic; four days old and already nicely padded with blubber, it could exist for quite a while without food. Pups who have become separated from their mothers due to rapidly moving ice in storm and current, or whose mothers have been killed by man or ice, can survive if they have been amply fed and are about a week old. Younger ones rarely make it. They cry and crawl, become progressively weaker, whimper for food and warmth, and die. Older pups have a better chance, but these starvelings remain stunted. Instead of moulting two weeks after birth, their ragged, rumpled natal coat clings to them for a month or more; while pups nursed for the normal two weeks weigh a plump 80 pounds and look like furry blimps, these pathetic waifs weigh barely 20. "Nogg-heads," Newfoundland sealers call them, for their heads appear large compared to their emaciated, spindly bodies.

The fatter a pup is at the time of weaning, the greater are its chances for survival. As if aware of this, it reacts to the first faint pangs of hunger with passionate wailing. The pup whose mother has not returned now shrills its need for food across the ice. It is famished and frantic. All around it females suckle their pups, or sleep near them, alluring dark shapes. The pup does not know its mother, is incapable of recognizing her. It creeps hopefully towards the nearest female. She rears up and trills her warning. Dismayed, the pup stops, but hunger and hope edge it on. The female's anger increases, the warning trill changes to a furious, snarly gurgle as the pup crawls over that invisible but to her very real line that demarcates her personal domain and distance. She makes rapid, flailing motions with her foreflipper. Normally, the pup would shy away from an enraged female, but now it is too desperate to heed the escalating warning signals. It moves a bit closer, the female rushes forward and gives it a buffet with her powerful foreflipper that bounces it, squalling, across the ice. Frightened but unhurt, it lies on the ice crying. Then, driven by the imperative need for food, it crawls towards the next female, only to be cuffed again, and on it creeps in its weary, anguished search. Finally, exhausted, it huddles, whimpering, next to a chunk of ice, a fluffy lump of abject misery.

Its mother has hauled out and searches for her pup. Purposefully, she goes to the spot where it had been. Since it is no longer there, she stops, baffled. She sniffs and listens. The pup is downwind from her; the breeze carries no familiar smell to her. She humps on, and argues with several females onto whose private ground she trespasses. She crosses the path of her pup and hesitates. Its smell is there but too faint to guide her. The pup begins to bleat again and at once the female moves with more assurance. She discovers it near the iceblock and sniffs it. The pup, with the memory of hard, painful cuffs from other females still in its mind, recoils in momentary fright. But the dark form does not threaten; its smell is vaguely familiar and comforting. The pup bawls loudly and nudges the female. She turns onto her side and the pup suckles greedily, urgently, changing frequently from one nipple to the other. The warm, rich milk fills its stomach, contentment suffuses its being. Its belly bulging, hushed and happy, it falls asleep near its mother.

Its stomach bulging with nutrient-rich milk, the pup relaxes on the ice.

Playfully, a pup wiggles in its bed of snow between ice floes.

Chapter four

Their Path Is In The Great Waters.

In summer and fall, the harp seals of the Gulf and Front herds had been scattered in small groups over an immensity of northern ocean, for to them, too, the psalmist's simile applies that their "way is in the sea and [their] path in the great waters," and they were spread over an area of more than a million square miles, along thousands of miles of arctic coast. They ranged along the fiord-serrated, food-rich, west coast of Greenland. They swam into inlets and bays that were flanked by lush green meadows dotted with grazing sheep, where centuries before the ill-fated Norse colonists had tended their flocks and built their homes of stone and sod. They swam past strange, metallic islands that clanked and groaned and wheezed as men searching for oil drilled into the ocean floor, and the seals gave them a wide berth, for the noises carried far in the water and were alien and frightening. They frolicked in Disko Bay through water as speckled with planktonic life as a shaft of sunlight with motes of dust. Elegant arctic terns hovered above the water on rapidly-beating wings, plunged like plumed arrows, emerged with tiny glittering fish held in stiletto beaks and flew off to their nesting colonies on the Green Islands.

Many groups of adult harp seals, and some immatures, had been even further north, in Melville Bay, where over a distance of nearly 200 miles giant glaciers flow from Greenland's two-mile-thick ice cap into the sea. With a noise of distant thunder, enormous icebergs broke off and floated out into the dark water, sea-borne alabaster peaks.

A few pods of harp seals ventured into the northernmost reaches of Baffin Bay. They swam past ice-riven cliffs banked by 500-foot talus slopes of frost-shattered rock, past immense snow fields tinted rose by a flush of sun-warmed algae growing upon them. They swam in the clear, soft light of the arctic night past sheer-cliffed, bird-dotted Hakluyt Island, and the sea was smooth and satiny, shimmering with an opalescent glow. Thousands of murres lay upon the still water and murmured and mumbled, and when the seals passed near them, they dipped forward and dived, throwing up little silvery splashes. Schools of milky-white whales slid through the dark sea with smooth, even strokes of their heart-shaped flukes and squeaked and trilled and grunted in a pleased and self-satisfied manner. Brownish, scarlet-rimmed jellyfish pulsed through the water, their diaphanous mantles expanding and contracting, and small, black, winged pelagic snails wafted along with measured beat. 'Tulugarssaq' the Polar Eskimos call them, the ones that look like ravens.

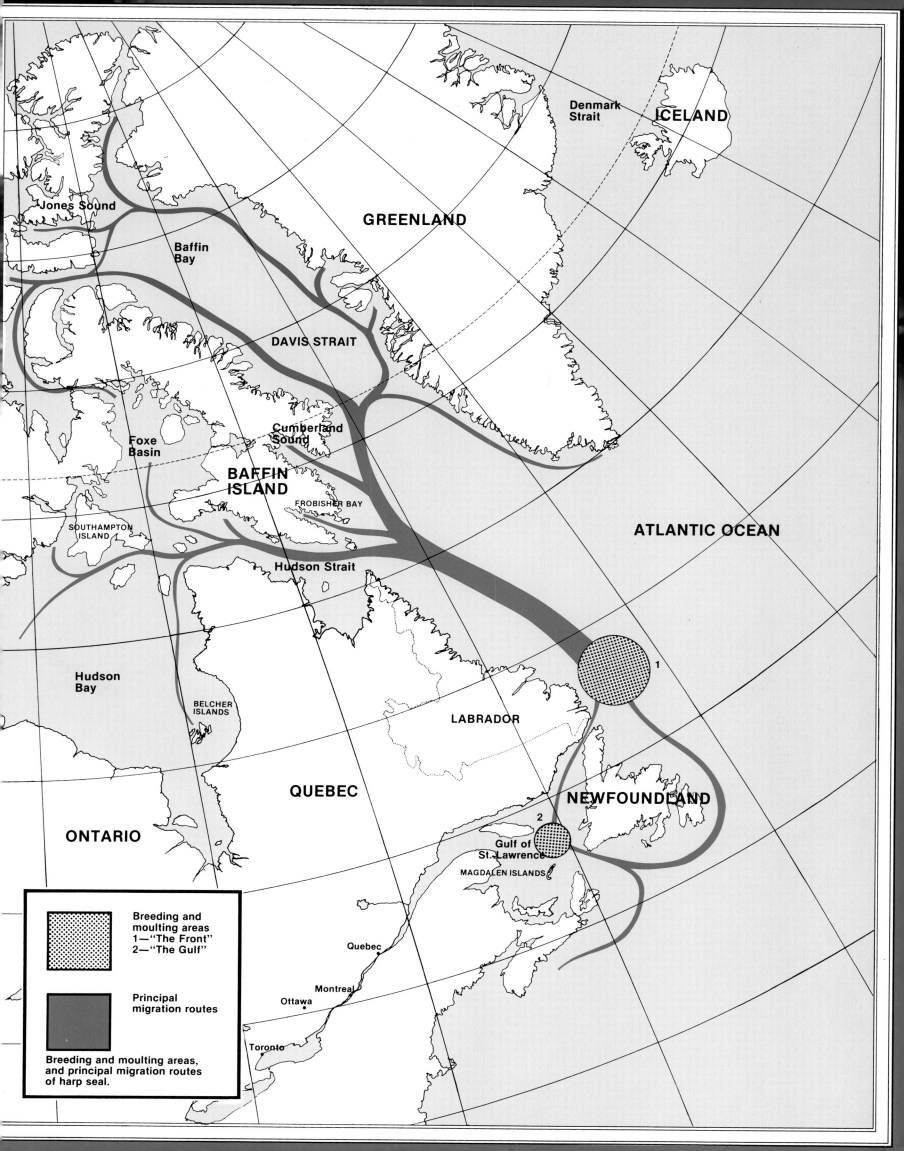

Denmark Strait

ICELAND

Jones Sound

GREENLAND

Baffin
Bay

DAVIS STRAIT

Foxe
Basin

Cumberland
Sound

BAFFIN
ISLAND

FROBISHER BAY

ATLANTIC OCEAN

SOUTHAMPTON
ISLAND

Hudson Strait

Hudson
Bay

BELCHER
ISLANDS

LABRADOR

1

QUEBEC

NEWFOUNDLAND

ONTARIO

2

Gulf of
St. Lawrence

MAGDALEN ISLANDS

Quebec

Montreal

Ottawa

Toronto

Breeding and
moulting areas
1—"The Front"
2—"The Gulf"

Principal
migration routes

Breeding and moulting areas,
and principal migration routes
of harp seal.

Soft-eyed but alert, a female takes a wary
glance over edge of floe.

Near Smith Sound, named by William Baffin in 1616 for one of his expedition patrons, Sir Thomas Smith, the seals reached vast fields of scattered ice floes. A lovely, melodic sound rang through the water, as of distant, delicate bells. Incongruously, it emanated from one of the massive, warty walrus bulls floating among the floes, its bulbous pharyngeal pouches acting as resonators. The seals skirted the walrus groups. They were not really afraid of them, just wary, for while the great majority of walruses are placid, harmless shellfish eaters, the odd one is a dangerous, deadly rogue, a killer that preys primarily on seals. Such walruses were probably orphaned while still young. They survived by feeding on carrion, developed a taste for meat and, fully grown, killed and ate seals. A rogue walrus swims stealthily up to a sleeping seal, enfolds it in deadly embrace with its powerful two-foot-long front flippers, crushes it, rips it with its tusks and strips the carcass of blubber and meat.

The sea among the floes was dotted with dovekies, starling-sized chubby seabirds that nest in millions in clefts and crevices among the rocks and boulders of the enormous scree slopes flanking Smith Sound. A pod of swift-swimming narwhal surged past the leisurely idling seals, the long, tapered, twisted ivory tusks of the males flashing through the water.

On right:
Harp seal mother casts a long shadow
as she threatens intruder.

Other groups of harp seals, after following first the Greenland coast toward the north, had then turned west to cross Baffin Bay with the receding ice and had spread into that vast labyrinth of straits, sounds, inlets, channels and gulfs of the Canadian arctic archipelago. They swam past Coburg Island, its cliffs crowded with 200,000 gabby murres, into Jones Sound, along the brooding, sienna-streaked mountains of Ellesmere Island. They rushed through fish-rich Lancaster Sound and turned north into Wellington Channel, swimming past Beechey Island, which the Eskimos call 'Iluvialu,' the island of graves, for here some members of Franklin's doomed expedition are buried. They swam along the coast of Baffin Island and into its innumerable fiords and sounds, flanked by rugged mountains, snow-streaked even in late summer. And some swam through Hudson Strait, past the soaring cliffs of Cape Wolstenholme that are streaked with green moss and bright-orange lichen well fertilized by half a million murres, and on into Hudson Bay.

Thus, although the harp seals of the Gulf and Front herds number about a million, and once numbered more than ten, they are dispersed in summer and fall over an area so vast, competition for food in any one region tends to be minimal. In October and November, as the northern sea begins to congeal in winter's grip, the seals swim south, and in late winter this scattered host converges upon the ice fields in the Gulf and on the Front, to pup, to mate and, later, to moult.

The young female seal swims beneath the ice with languid ease. On the ice she had been slow and ungainly in motion, flabby and flaccid in repose. She can cope with the ice, but her real realm is the sea with which she melds in perfect harmony.

In water, her blubber buoys her, she is part of the sea, nearly weightless she drifts through it with supple grace. When she sleeps, she hangs suspended in the water, just beneath the surface, like a slightly weighted floating bottle. Every five minutes or so, her body signals its need for oxygen to the brain. It sends a message to the rear flipper muscles, they flex and contract, a few slight strokes send her to the surface, she breathes, renewing her body's oxygen supply, the flipper movements cease, and she sinks slowly beneath the surface, still sound asleep. She follows the same breathing rhythm when hauled out on the ice. For many minutes she lies as still as a leaden lump; suddenly her tightly closed nostrils flare, she breathes deeply, rapidly, and sinks again into apparent inertia.

She is a warm-blooded, air-breathing mammal. Her lungs are proportionately not bigger than those of a human, yet she can stay submerged for nearly 30 minutes while a human can barely manage two. She can dive to the crushing depth of 600 feet and more, and she can rise from this depth with a rapidity that would be fatal to any human diver, who would die of the bends, the dreaded, excruciatingly painful caisson disease. She is a marvel of marine design, flouting with impunity the apparent limitations imposed upon her by her land ancestry. Nature has not equipped her with special organs, she has merely modified and perfected those of her terrestrial forebears to give them superlative efficiency in the sea.

To live, both man and seal require oxygen. They are mammals and, unlike fish, cannot absorb oxygen from the water. They must take it with them when they dive. Within less than a minute of submerging, carbon dioxide begins to build up in the human diver's blood, urgent signals flash to his brain and trigger there the alarm symptoms of imminent suffocation. It is an early warning system and a trained diver can stay down about another minute. By then the oxygen supply of his body is dangerously depleted and he must surface to breathe.

On right:
Bobbing out of the water,
a seal scans the horizon.

The young female seal displays her adaptive superiority already when she breathes. A human renews the air in his lungs only partially with each breath, the seal renews it nearly completely. She can restore her oxygen supply within seconds after a short dive, and usually within about two minutes after a dive that lasted nearly half an hour. The instant she dives, she expels the air from her lungs, but she carries in her body considerably more oxygen than a human could, and she husbands this supply with much greater efficiency during her prolonged dive.

As the seal dives, her heartbeat slows from the normal 115 beats per minute to only 10 per minute. Her peripheral vascular system constricts; the oxygenated blood is reserved for priority regions of her body, the brain and vital organs. She carries oxygen not only in the haemoglobin of her blood cells (and her body contains, proportionally, half again as much blood as the human body), but also in the myoglobin of her muscles. Her body draws upon these oxygen reserves sparingly, tolerates a high carbon dioxide concentration and, when the supplies are nearly exhausted runs up, in a marvel of body chemistry, an "oxygen debt," which she repays by rapid oxygenation the next time she surfaces. Then, for a few moments, her heart which had been idling while she had been submerged, races wildly, flushing her body with oxygen-rich blood, to be stored for the next dive.

As the seal dives down, ever down, on a slanting trajectory toward the eerie darkness of the abyss, she is subjected to awesome pressure: nearly 300 pounds for every square inch of her body at a depth of 600 feet. At this depth, a human diver would be dead, his ribs broken, his chest collapsed, his lungs ruptured. The seal, partially protected by her thick blubber coat, also has ribs that are flexible, they bend but do not break. Her lungs, emptied before she dived, fold until they are nearly flat. What little air is left in them is forced into the tough and pliant, less absorptive regions of the bronchi. She drifts through the deep in search of prey, then ascends rapidly to the surface to breathe.

She is a creature of the sea; its three-dimensional vastness surrounds her with a myriad signs, and sounds and signals which her senses, superbly attuned, absorb, her brain decodes, to which her body reacts. She is immersed in a totality of subtle sensations that guide her and warn her, to which she responds partly with the innate knowledge of her race, acquired, tested and perfected through millions of years, partly through experience gained in her own brief lifetime while swimming and hunting through tens of thousands of miles of sea.

Her eyes are a miracle of adaptation to the exigencies of two optically different mediums, and to the extremes of light and dark. She sees adequately in air and can endure the scintillating glare upon the ice. And she can dive far down into the sea and pursue fish in the darkness of the deep. The instant she dives, powerful dilator muscles open wide the pupils of her large eyes. A film of fine, clear oil, constantly renewed, protects her eyes from irritation by water; their corneas have the same refractive index as water and she sees without distortion. Her retinas are extremely light sensitive and this is further enhanced by the tapetum lucidum, layers of silvery crystals behind the retina that reflect and amplify ambient light, projecting it upon the retina's receptor cells. Much of her life is spent in the dim twilight zones of the sea. Where man would barely be able to discern a shape at close range, she hunts quick-darting fish with speed and assurance.

A harp seal has caught a sculpin. The spiny fish is hard to swallow and the seal comes onto the ice to deal with its prickly prey.

She does not rely on vision alone. Infinitely fine fluctuations in water pressure, the ripples of turbulence created by fleeing fish, the lap of water against blocks of ice pressed far beneath the floes, are picked up by her whiskers. Folded close to her face when she lies on the ice, the stiff whiskers stand abristle when she dives and receive, like sensitive antennae, the minute but telltale vibrations of the sea.

She swims through a world of sound, for the sea is not silent and her hearing is acute. Sound waves move more than four times faster in water than in air, and sounds travel much farther. The great whales can communicate in the sea across tens, perhaps hundreds, of miles. When men walked on the ice, the young female seal could clearly hear the creak and groan of the snow beneath their boots although she was swimming more than a mile away. A human diver would have heard the same noise, though not at such a distance for his hearing is not nearly as sharp as a seal's. He would have felt surrounded by sound, enveloped in sound, diffuse and all-pervading. He would have been incapable of indicating the source of the sound which to him appears to come evenly from all sides, for in water man is bereft of directional hearing.

The seal has no external ear to break the smooth flow of her head. A few inches behind the eye, there is a tiny otic opening leading to the meatus, a pin-thin auditory canal. When the seal surfaces, the meatus opens, sound waves reach the eardrum, cause it to vibrate and the seal hears in the same physiological fashion as a human and about as well, if not better. But when she dives, muscles and water pressure close the meatus. Yet despite this she hears the vibrant voices of the sea with total clarity. In some marvellous, mysterious way the water-borne sound waves strike the outer opening of the meatus and continue, by a process of conduction, inward through fibre, bone and cartilage, to bring their messages to the auditory nerves. The sound waves reach each inner ear separately and the seal's directional hearing is excellent.

The young female slides through the water with steady, even strokes of her broad, webbed rear flippers. She is as one with the sea, she glides through it in perfect sensuous harmony. But when she must leave the sea, to moult, or when her pup will be born on the ice, then she and her kind are at the mercy of man.

Above:
One-week old harp seal pups on the ice
of the Gulf of St. Lawrence.

A moulting pup among the ice blocks of the Gulf.

Chapter five
The Way It Used To Be.

Four times in the million-year period of the Pleistocene, giant glaciers, in some places two miles thick, grooved and gouged their way southward across the primeval Precambrian rocks of the Canadian Shield. And four times the carapace of ice retreated, leaving the land strewn with till and seamed with eskers and moraines. Lichen and moss crept cautiously over the naked land; hardy tundra plants followed, bloomed, died and decayed, and slowly, ever so slowly, at the rate of half an inch every five hundred years, soil accumulated and covered the ice-scoured rocks. Trees sprouted, sending out their tentacle-like roots laterally to seek sustenance from the meager soil, creeping into every crevice to anchor themselves to this hostile, wind-swept land, and in time vast, brooding forests of spruce and pine and fir covered much of the interior of Newfoundland and Labrador.

No gentle Gulf Stream caresses these shores; the Labrador Current hugs them with its icy, arctic waters. Vicious storms lash the gaunt, grey coast, its forest a tangle of twisted, stunted trees. Immense ice fields press and grind against the shore. Grey fog rolls in from a lead-grey sea. "This is the land God gave to Cain," wrote Jacques Cartier when he saw the south Labrador coast in 1534. "[It] is composed of stones and horrible rugged rock ... there is nothing but moss and short stunted shrub."

Sir Humfry Gilbert claimed Newfoundland for England in 1583, but he was not favorably impressed. The coast, he noted, consists of "hideous rocks and mountains, bare of trees, and voide of any greene herbe," and to his friend, the historian Richard Hakluyt he wrote: "I see nothing but solitude." A sentiment shared by a disgruntled 19th century traveller who wrote home that Newfoundland is "nought but a land of fogs, bogs and dogs."

The Spanish cartographer Ribero dealt with Labrador on his 1529 map in two terse sentences: "Labrador was discovered by the English. There is nothing in it of any value." He was wrong on both counts. The first Europeans to visit Labrador were the Norsemen. They called it Markland, the forest land. And the land, and above all the sea, contained a vast wealth. John Cabot, after discovering Newfoundland in 1497, reported that "the sea there is swarming with fish," so numerous, they could be hauled up in weighted wicker baskets. The news spread fast. When Sir Humfry Gilbert sailed into St. John's in 1583, to claim Newfoundland for England, he found there 36 fishing ships, 20 Spanish and Portuguese and 16 from France and England, all attracted by the "inexhaustible supply of fish." The explorer John Davis, searching unsuccessfully for the Northwest Passage in 1586, found along the Labrador coast of "foule and fish mighty store," and these were "the largest and best fed fish that ever I sawe."

Harp seal mothers and pups on the ice in the Gulf of St. Lawrence and, right, on the "Front ice" off northern Newfoundland.

In the rivers of Labrador "salmon innumerable were leaping into the air," reported Captain George Cartwright in the 1780s. In June and July spawning capelin came to shore in shoals so dense, fishermen ladled them out of the surf with dipnets, and children carried them ashore in buckets. Polar bears and black bears were common, and more than a million caribou roamed the wilds of Labrador. Of whales there was "greate store" and, as the explorer William Baffin pointed out in 1616 "... easie to be strooke, because they are not used to be chased or beaten." Audubon, in 1833, stopped for a day on the west coast of Newfoundland and within a few hours his crew picked up, at low tide, 99 large lobsters among rocks in shallow water. "... the shores truly abound" with them, he noted in his journal.

Sea and land were infinitely rich in birds. Jacques Cartier landed on Funk Island, off Newfoundland, home to the stately, nearly three-foot tall, flightless great auks in 1534 and again in 1535. "This island is so exceedingly full of birds that all the ships of France might load a cargo of them without one perceiving that any had been removed," he wrote. Augustin Le Gardeur de Courtemanche, to whom Louis XIV gave the concession of Labrador, "the country of the wild Eskimos," in 1689, made a survey of his realm in 1704. "The islands and islets are covered with birds," particularly eider ducks, he reported happily. And in fall the Eskimo curlews returned from the north. Audubon saw the vanguard of the great migration at Blanc Sablon on Belle Isle Strait in 1833. It reminded him of the multi-million bird flocks of passenger pigeons. "The accounts given of these Curlews border on the miraculous," he wrote. The naturalist A.S. Packard saw the curlews on the Labrador coast in August of 1860: "We saw one flock which may have been a mile long and nearly as broad ... their notes sounded at times like the wind whistling through the ropes of a thousand-ton ship." They were so fat, New Englanders called them "dough birds."

Pup's attention is focused on its
approaching mother.

Laboriously, a harp seal mother humps
across the wind-sculptured snow to the
spot where she left her pup.

Bewhiskered and curious, a harp seal
surfaces in a lead among the floes.

In fall, too, the harp seals returned from the north, perhaps ten million strong. About 1760, a French settler saw them pass near the north tip of Newfoundland, and they filled the sea from shore to horizon for ten days and nights.

This immense animal wealth was ruthlessly exploited. Funk Island became the larder of the fishing fleets. In 1578, 350 Spanish and French and 50 English vessels fished near it, and the fishermen, a contemporary account notes "doe bring small store of flesh with them, but victuall themselves always with these birds." It was so easy. On land the great auk was slow and helpless. "When the water is smooth, they [the fishermen] make their shallops fast to the shore, lay gang-boards from the gunwale to the rocks and then drive as many penguins [great auks] on board as she will hold," reported Captain George Cartwright. In the late 18th century, feathers became an important trade item. Men camped on Funk Island all summer, herded the auks into pounds, bludgeoned them to death and parboiled them in great cauldrons to loosen the feathers. By 1800 the great auk was extinct on Funk Island. The last great auks in the world were killed on Eldey Island, off Iceland, on June 3, 1844. The men sold the remains of the two auks for $9. Now a great auk skin is worth about $8,000.

The Eskimo curlews that flew along the Labrador coast, according to a Smithonian Institution report, "in millions that darkened the sky" were also shot and clubbed in millions. They are now considered "virtually extinct." Polar bears vanished from the Labrador coast; walruses were exterminated; caribou became rare. Near Blanc Sablon on Belle Isle Strait, ducks were killed in "incredible numbers," Courtemanche noted in 1704. A century later the infamous 'eggers' descended upon the Labrador coasts. They methodically destroyed all eggs on the islands, then returned to collect the fresh ones. The egger, Audubon wrote in 1833, "gathers and gathers until he has swept the rocks bare. The dollars alone chink in his sordid mind ... This war of extermination cannot last many years more ...." Most species survived, though greatly depleted, but the strikingly-colored Labrador duck was extinct by 1875.

As the result of "the enormous destruction of everything here .. the aborigines themselves [are] melting away before the encroachment of the white man," Audubon wrote in his journal. "For as the Deer, the Caribou, and all other game is killed for the dollar ... the Indian must search in vain over the devastated country ... [the Indian dies for] want of food, the loss of hope as he loses sight of all that was once abundant."

With flippers too short to reach very far, pups get at those itchy places by twisting against piled up ice.

A young female harp seal on the Gulf ice.

At the time of Audubon's visit, Newfoundland's Indians, the Beothuk, were already extinct. Their calvary began in 1501, when the Portuguese explorer Gaspar Corte-Réal returned with 57 caught in Newfoundland. The Venetian ambassador to Portugal inspected the captives and reported: "... they are gentle ... and better made in the legs, arms and shoulders, than is possible to describe ... His Serene Majesty [King Manuel of Portugal] anticipates the greatest advantage from this country ... [for the people that inhabit it] appear admirably fitted to endure labour, and will probably turn out the best slaves that have been discovered up to this time." That scheme fell through, but "Indian hunting" became a popular diversion for Newfoundland's European settlers. The trapper Noel Boss boasted that he had killed 99 men, women and children. Children were occasionally captured and sold as exhibits to fairs and menageries, but the general policy, a contemporary report notes, was to "kill the nits with the lice." The settlers shot the adult Indians, then rounded up the children and cut their throats. The last Beothuk, Nancy April (so called because she had been captured in April), died in the spring of 1829.

The Eskimos along the coast of southern Labrador suffered the same fate. Sea hunters, they had been attracted to this region by its great wealth in seals, seabirds and fish. The advent of European fishermen started hostilities. The "war" began, according to Champlain, early in the 17th century with "the killing — accidental or otherwise — of a wife of a chief of that nation by one of the St. Malo sailors." Unlike the meeker Beothuk, the Eskimos fought back and, consequently, wrote Sir Hugh Palliser, governor of Newfoundland, in 1766 they were "considered in no other light than as thieves and murderers" and, as a rule, were shot on sight. The odds were against them. In 1766, 1,500 European vessels with 15,000 men caught fish off the south Labrador coast. Inexorably, the Eskimos along this coast were exterminated; the survivors fled towards the north. There the Moravian Brethren from Germany established their first mission at Nain in 1771, and others in quick succession. Although from then on the Labrador Eskimos lived in peace, their existence was haunted by a new scourge: European diseases to which they had little resistance and immunity.

Sadly, and in meticulous Gothic script, the Moravian missionaries recorded the decline of their flock in their voluminous, vellum-bound diaries: Okak, 1850: fifty Eskimos die in an epidemic. Hebron, 1863: fifty people die in six months. Nain, 1894: close to 100 people die of a population of 250. Nain, 1902, [at the death of a child]: "We were sorry to hear of his loss, as this is the last of 13 children his wife has borne." Hopedale, 1907: "There is no doubt of the sad fact that the Eskimo race is dying out in Labrador." In 1918 a sick sailor aboard the supply ship *Harmony* brought the Spanish 'flu' to Labrador. In Hebron, "in the course of nine days two-thirds of the ... population were corpses." In Okak 215 died of a population of 263. "The entire male population has been wiped out."

Weighing only 18 pounds at birth, the pups triple their weight in two weeks.

European settlement of Newfoundland and Labrador proceeded slowly because vested English interests frowned on it. For English ship owners, ship builders, merchants and chandlers, the Newfoundland-Labrador fishery was a lucrative business and they obdurately opposed settlement of "the newe founde lande." The English government agreed with this point of view, in part because it regarded the fishery as an excellent training school for English sailors who could, in time of need, be pressed into service in the Royal Navy. As late as the latter part of the 18th century, Admiral Palliser received instructions from the English government that "It is the King's intention to reserve the whole of the new possessions for English adventurers ... Any Newfoundlanders going to Labrador to fish will be flogged ..."

Despite such edicts and threats, settlers spread out along the shores of Newfoundland and later to Labrador, living in small hamlets, always near the sea, on this bleak and blustery coast. Some of the more remote villages were extremely isolated. Queen Victoria died in February 1901. The people of Hopedale in Labrador did not hear about it until August of that year.

The names they gave to this harsh and rugged coast reflect the life and the spirit of the settlers. Some names were lyric: Ireland's Eye, Rose-au-Rue, Spanish Room, Happy Valley, Happy Adventure, Heart's Desire, Heart's Delight and Heart's Content. Some were tempestuous: Blow Hard Island, Blow-Me-Down Mountain and Slambang Bay. Some were mischievously derisive: Misfit Island, Witless Bay, Dumbell Island. Some showed a puckish delight in the geographical pun: Seal Bight, Lush's Bight, Shark Gut, Horse Chops, Lord's Arm, Famish Gut and Cutthroat Tickle. And many mirrored the loneliness and hardships of the settlers' existence: Starvation Island, Seldom-Come-By, Breakheart Point, Wrecked Boat Island, Coldfeet Rocks, Bareneed, and Nothing Bay.

Cod was king. Its importance, and smell, permeated all Newfoundland life. "For dirt and filth of all kinds St. John's may, in my opinion, reign unrivalled," wrote Sir Joseph Banks of Britain's prestigious Royal Society after visiting Newfoundland in 1766.

Steering with front flippers, harp seals swim towards "bobbing holes" to surface and breathe.

"As everything here smells of fish, so you cannot get anything that does not taste of it." The islanders' staple winter food was dried cod, eaten with seal oil and cranberries, a mixture known as 'pipsey.' They fished along the coast from home-built, open boats or, in summer, went "down to the Labrador." (Newfoundlanders say "down north" and "up south.") By 1802, 1,000 vessels were catching fish off the Labrador coast. The people who went to Labrador were 'Planters,' 'Floaters' and 'Liveyeres.' The Planters (or Stationers) came in summer with their families to operate shore fishing stations, living in flimsy shacks called 'tilts.' The Floaters were ship-based fishermen. And the Liveyeres (the people who "live 'ere") settled on the Labrador coast.

These settlers in Newfoundland and Labrador, mostly of English, Scottish and Irish descent, were a hardy, proud, independent-minded people. But their independence was illusory, for they were held in virtual bondage by an evil system of exploitation. They worked incredibly hard, but the merchants who controlled the market paid little for their produce, yet sold the goods the fishermen needed at exorbitant prices. As a result most fishermen were forever in debt to the merchants. It was a system in which the merchants held all the trumps and they prospered pleasantly. R.H. Bonnycastle, an English officer stationed in Newfoundland, observed in 1842 "a finer, healthier, or better educated and behaved colonial 'gentry' there does not exist." But he also noted "the extreme wretchedness of the accommodation of the very poor ... [who] are somewhat numerous," but, fortunately, he observed "they are not clamorous."

They lived, wrote the English traveller A.C. Laut in 1899 "in little dilapidated cottages ... Men, women, and children have scarcely enough clothing to hide their nakedness." The man works "for six toilsome, hazardous months ... [fifteen hours each day from May] till October when clothes and nets stiffen in the freezing spray. And fifteen or sixteen dollars ... [are] his sole reward." Rev. Julian Morton, minister at Greenspond in the 19th century wrote of the fishermen's houses: "Aged people, having but languid circulation, are liable to frost-burning in their beds." Only by "hunting seals in spring" Laut noted, could many fishermen survive.

Almost immobile, a pup cranes for a better view.

In late November and in December ice begins to form off Labrador and northern Newfoundland. The sea seems to steam; greyish whisps of moisture swirl up into the icy air. Ice crystals form in the rapidly cooling water, and the swells run oily and sluggish. The crystals coalesce and grow into round floes of pancake ice that dapple the dark sea. Wind and waves twist and turn the pans, grind them together and pull them apart, and mounds of milky mush rim the floes. At the same time the current-carried polar pack descends from the north, massive floes of hard, deep-blue ice, often five feet thick. Northeasterly gales force the ice masses against unyielding shores; the ice fields compact, floes rafter, buckle and tilt, and rear up into chaotic pressure ridges.

Westerly storms drive the vast ice fields, that extend over thousands of square miles, out to sea. The pressure slackens. The floes pull apart. Swells from the open sea run beneath the floes, and the great expanse of ice rises and falls like an immense undulating white carpet. The pans collide and churn and turn, they groan and screech and creak. (John Davis, the Elizabethan explorer, came upon the pack ice in dense fog in 1586 and heard from afar the "mighty great roaring of the sea ... [caused] by the rouling of this yce together.")

This is the "Front Ice," the precarious nursery of the harp seals. Here, in the first days of March (about a week later than the harp seals in the Gulf) the females haul out and give birth to their pups on the floes. On a rare calm day, this floating world of ice can be breathtakingly beautiful. But when one of the frequent late-winter storms shrieks over the ice and sets the monstrous mass in motion, when conflicting forces of current, waves and wind begin to twist the floes, so that they gyrate and screw, then it becomes a harrowing world of chaos and tumult, and often thousands of pups, helpless on the ice, are killed by overriding floes and tumbling ice blocks.

The seals, having spent summer and fall in food-rich regions of the far north, swim southward ahead of the advancing ice. They follow the coast of Labrador. A young English trader on the Labrador coast, Lambert de Boilieu saw the seals pass in the 1850s and wrote: "To mark a shoal of these animals ... quietly swimming, with head and part of the shoulder out of the water — the head being a jetty black and the shoulder tinged with silver lustre — the coal-black eye shining ... like a diamond, is a magnificent sight indeed. I have often felt ... remorse when killing these animals, there is such a human expressiveness in their eye ..."

Harp seal mother and pup on glistening Gulf ice.

Near Belle Isle, the throng divides: about a third of the seals swims through Belle Isle Strait into the Gulf of St. Lawrence, the others follow the east coast of Newfoundland and scatter over the vastness of the Grand Banks. Long ago, Eskimos hunted them with kayaks and nets. Later European settlers of both the Labrador coast and northern Newfoundland set nets to trap the migrating seals, or went out in boats to shoot them. By the end of the 18th century, the seals ran a gauntlet of about 2,000 nets set all along the coasts to intercept them. Most were simple "shoal nets," large-meshed and made of strong twine, set at right angles to shore or across a strategic tickle or gut, favored by passing seals. A few, such as the "great fishery" used by the Robertson family of La Tabatière on the south shore of Labrador from the beginning of the 19th century to the present day, consisted of an immense, intricate maze of mesh-enclosed funnels and chambers, made out of one-and-a-half tons of twine and rope.

To the settlers the seals were of vital importance: they ate the meat and fed it to their sled dogs; they used seal oil with their food and burned it in their lamps; they wore caps, boots and jackets made of sealskin; and the surplus of skins and oil they sold. Occasionally onshore winds packed the seals' whelping ice onto the coast and men from all the adjacent villages scrambled over the floes to kill harp seal pups, the "whitecoats," and lugged the sculps, the skin plus the thick underlying layer of blubber, to shore.

But the seal herds then were enormous, and the shore fishermen's catch minimal. Starting around 1800 this changed. Men took boats to the ice to kill the seals and their pups. Soon thousands of men in hundreds of ships were killing millions of seals. The seal fishery became a great industry. At its peak it employed 13,000, more than half of Newfoundland's able-bodied men. It brought death and disaster to many, and wealth to a fortunate few, who wisely never went sealing.

It's instant recognition for young pup and mother.

*Despite those soulful eyes, many a pup
meets early death at the hands of man.*

Chapter six
"The Sea Is Made Of Mothers' Tears."

"All seal hunting is mean, merciless slaughter in which cruelty and insensitivity join... The oil... and fur of seals are sought-after articles... [and this explains] to some extent... man's mania to annihilate these animals," wrote the famous 19th century biologist Alfred Brehm. During that century sealing reached its apogee and sealers roamed the globe in search of their valuable prey. They depleted most species. A few they hunted to near-extinction.

Between 1800 and 1900, more than three million northern fur seals, breeding on isolated, fog-shrouded islands in the Bering Sea, were killed. At the turn of the century about 200,000 remained. The southern fur seals fared worse. When the Russian explorer Fabian von Bellingshausen sailed along what he assumed to be unknown coasts of Antarctica in 1821, he was chagrined to find that the area was already being systematically exploited by American and British sealers. Wiping out rookery after rookery on island after island they killed, from 1822 on, an average of a million fur seals each year. Within less than a decade the southern fur seals had been nearly exterminated. The massive southern elephant seals were shot by hundreds of thousands and their blubber rendered into oil. By 1900 so few remained, the hunt, no longer profitable, was abandoned. Of the once-great herds of northern elephant seals only about 100 animals were left by 1900. The Pacific walrus once numbered about 300,000. Between 1860 and 1880 alone, commercial walrus hunters killed more than 200,000. The Guadalupe fur seal was slaughtered in millions. By 1900 it was thought to be extinct. But a few, breeding and hiding in remote caves, survived the massacre and they have now increased to about 600.

Above:
Harp seal pups, the "whitecoats" of sealers, are killed for their fur and fat.

Most numerous of all were the harp seals. Two centuries ago when the females hauled out to give birth to their pups, hundreds of square miles of ice were dotted with their dark shapes. And the hunt of the harp seals has no equal. It has now lasted nearly two hundred years, and about fifty to sixty million seals have been killed of the Front and Gulf herds alone. If one adds to this the killed harp seals of the two other herds — the one east of Greenland, the other in Russia's White Sea — the total rises to about 70 million, the greatest, most protracted mass slaughter ever inflicted upon any wild mammal species. The men who took part in the hunt endured incredible hardships and danger; more than a thousand died and thousands more were maimed. Yet they went willingly, eagerly, for a meager reward, as men go to war. After the toil of summer fishing and the tedium of winter in poorly heated homes, the great seal hunt was their primeval rite of spring, its powerful allure composed of shared adventure and danger and thrill in the kill. Oppressed by grey and grinding poverty, they found relief in the wild and bloody exhilaration of the hunt. "The annual seal hunt of Newfoundland is one great carnival of cruelty and bloodshed," noted the writer Beckles Willson.

Until about 1800, the Newfoundland harp seal "fishery" was a modest enterprise. Migrating seals were caught in nets and in years when the ice was pressed against the coast by onshore winds, men from the nearest villages made forays to the ice to kill harp seal pups. In such years, they might kill tens of thousands of seals, but usually the take was much smaller. In 1795, they killed only 4,900 harp seals. Tantalizing, beyond their grasp as long as they operated from shore, was the immense breeding pack, nursery to millions of seals. The "West Ice" herd near the island of Jan Mayen off East Greenland was already being exploited. In 1760, 19 vessels from Hamburg took part in the hunt and returned with 45,000 seals. Fourteen years later, 54 ships, mostly Dutch and German, were sealing among the storm-haunted floes of the "West Ice." Demand for seal products was high, and remained high throughout the 19th century.

Since 1800, millions of harp seal pups have been killed.

The thick blubber of adult seals and pups was rendered into a pure, clear, tasteless, odorless oil. It was used in the manufacture of soap and ointments and perfumes. It was important as a lubricating oil to keep the new-fangled machinery of the industrial revolution running smoothly, and later it was used in the production of margarine. Prior to being replaced by technology's newest child, kerosene, whale oil and, to a lesser extent, seal oil lit the lamps of Europe and America: in homes, on the streets, deep down in the mines, and high in the glowing beacons of lighthouses. Seal skins were turned into leather. Ladies' handbags were made from it, the satchels of school children, and cigar cases for the men. "Pinseal" leather, made from the pups' skins, was popular for elegant pocket-books and wallets, and was also used extensively in bookbinding. The saddles of the first bicycles were moulded from seal leather and so, later, were many of the popular, patent leather pumps. The demand was there, the seals were there in millions, and New-foundland's outports were home to fishermen renowned for their hardiness and daring.

They began to follow the seals, first in open row-ing boats, then in partly-decked 30-foot sailing shallops, with crews of from five to ten men, and later in schooners and brigs that ranged from 80 to 200 tons, with an average crew of 35 men. These were sturdy vessels, most of them built in the outports. Their number rose fast. In 1805, 81 ships took part in the hunt and they returned with more than 80,000 seals. Ten years later, 126 ships sailed to the ice; in 1830 they numbered 558 and in 1840 the greatest sealing fleet ever, 631 vessels, converged upon the immense ice fields. That year, they killed more than 600,000 seals. But the all-time peak had already been attained in 1831, when the Newfoundland sealers returned with 686,000 sculps, sealskins with the underlying layer of blubber.

The hunt was hard and dangerous. Most of the sailing ships had no stoves, no galleys. When men fell into the icy water, a common occurrence, they con-tinued to hunt in their sodden clothes, and then slept in them, since there was nowhere to dry them. There were no hot meals to warm them. For weeks they sub-sisted on hardtack and raw seal meat. As the hunt proceeded, the ships became coated with grime and grease. "You can smell a sealer almost as far as you can see him," the famous sealing captain Robert (Bob) Bartlett acknowledged. Holds were crammed with sculps and the sealers slept on the reeking pelts. Their clothes became saturated with oil and blood. "Greasy-jackets," sealers were called in New-foundland.

On right:
Struggling across the ice, a long file of
sealers hauls sculps to their ship.

The ships were stoutly built but they were no match for the might of the ice. The goal of every captain was to reach the "main patch," the greatest concentration of seals, usually far from the edge of the pack where the floes roller-coaster wildly after one of the frequent storms. So the sealers forced their way through the ice, followed leads, and cut the ice with great saws or blasted it with cans of powder when their ships got jammed. As long as westerly winds kept the ice slack, they were fairly safe. But when the wind swung to the northeast and forced the immense ice fields towards shore, the ice compacted, the ships were nipped between crashing, rafting floes, and many were crushed. Near the Wadhams, in 1852, 40 sealing ships were caught in ice driven upon shore. One by one their hulls crumpled and finally all were in splinters. Their crews, 1,500 men, scrambled across the floes and camped on the bleak, treeless islands until they were rescued. In 1861, 26 sealing vessels were crushed by ice in a bad storm. Another 140 were locked in by ice which held them captive for many weeks.

Altogether, more than 400 sailing ships were destroyed by ice during the 19th century off Newfoundland. Yet each spring, undaunted by the prospect of incredible hardships, certain danger and possible death, the men from the outports vied for a "berth" to the ice. The Newfoundland sealers, said the American writer George Allan England who went on a sealing voyage with them, are the "strongest, hardiest and bravest men I have ever known." To be a 'swiler,' a sealer, was to be truly a man. In 1857, 400 vessels with a total of 13,000 men went to the hunt. They killed nearly half a million seals that year, worth more than $1,200,000. And in the outports children sang that instead of:

"Maggoty fish...
there would be
"Cake and tea for breakfast,
Pork and duff for supper,
When daddy comes home from swilin'."

The hunt hardened the men. They were indifferent and inured to its cruelty. The seal pups that lie, as Sir Wilfred Grenfell wrote, "in a fluffy bed of snow, fanning themselves with their flippers in the sun, looking like large butterballs dressed in down," were to the sealers merely "fat," to be killed and sculped. The English geologist J.B. Jukes went along on a sailing sealer in 1840 and was appalled by the cruelty of the hunt. "In passing through a thin skirt of ice, one of the men hooked up a young seal with his gaff. Its cries were precisely like those of a young child in the extremity of agony and distress, something between shrieks and convulsive sobbings... I saw one poor wretch skinned... while yet alive, and the body writhing in blood after being stripped of its pelt ... In the bustle, hurry and excitement these things pass as a matter of course... but they are most horrible... The vision of one poor wretch writhing its snow-white woolly body with its head bathed in blood, through which it was vainly endeavouring to see and breathe, really haunted my dreams."

About the middle of the 19th century, with arctic whaling on the wane, whalers began to augment profits by joining in the seal hunt. In 1849, 42 British ships killed 218 whales and 50,000 seals. The following year they slaughtered 400,000 seals. That year the total harp seal kill of sealers and whalers exceeded one million!

Arctic whaling was then already an ancient industry. In 1607, England's Muscovy Company asked Henry Hudson to sail to Cathay via the North Pole. Ice stopped him at 81° N near Spitsbergen but he did find an abundance of whales in the area. They were Greenland right whales, the bowhead of the whalers, "which whale is the best of all sorts," the Muscovy Company happily noted. They were wrapped in a blanket of blubber nearly two feet thick, weighing 30 tons on a large bowhead, and it rendered into valuable oil. Its 600 to 800 baleen plates were ten to 13 feet long, weighed a total of nearly a ton, worth at one time $6 a pound. So valuable was baleen that a single bowhead whale could pay for a two-year whaling voyage. In 1848, Captain W.T. Walker took an ancient whaling ship, worth about $8,000, to Baffin Bay and returned six months later with a cargo worth $138,450.

Arctic whaling was hard, ruthless, frenetic and the profits, for that age, were astronomical. Between 1675 and 1721, the Dutch alone employed 5,886 ships in the Spitsbergen region, and took 32,907 whales with a gross value of $82,267,000!

By 1630, bowheads had been all but exterminated in the fiords of Spitsbergen. The hunt moved west, and during the next 70 years most of the bowheads between Spitsbergen and Greenland were slaughtered. In 1719, two Dutch ships discovered the whaling grounds of Davis Strait. Four years later, 350 ships took part in that hunt.

Swift-moving hunters have missed this pup among the jumbled ice.

Life aboard the whalers was grim. The crews were rough, the captains tough, and the conditions extremely hard. The crew was crammed into the tiny forecastle, dank, dark and verminous. The food was bad: 'salt horse' (dried salt-beef); 'dandy funk' (powdered hardtack and molasses); 'scouse' (stew of fat or pork and hardtack); and on Sundays 'plum duff,' made of flour, drippings and raisins and boiled for hours. When a voyage lasted long, scurvy became rampant. In 1837 the *Dee* returned to Aberdeen with nine alive of a crew of 46, and the *Advice* to Dundee with seven survivors of a crew of 49. Sometimes crews mutinied but whaling captains came prepared for trouble. Ship's provisions in 1870 included: six dozen pain-killer; three dozen rat exterminator; and twelve pairs handcuffs.

In addition, there was the hazard of the hunt. Dunkings in the icy water were frequent and unless fished out quickly, the men perished or suffered severe frostbite. Captain William Scoresby hauled out a man "his clothes frozen like mail, and his hair constituted a helmet of ice." In 1822, while rowing after a whale, the men of the *King George* were caught in a storm and returned drenched and frozen. That day their surgeon "amputated 35 fingers and toes." Later that year, the *King George* was crushed by ice. There were no survivors.

In the 1850s, Scottish whalers began to use steam ships, 300 to 400-ton vessels, built of hardwood throughout (mainly oak), sheathed with greenheart, their bows plated with steel. Between the interior timber and the shell was a layer of rock salt, to cushion the crushing blows of the ice, bringing the hull's total thickness to about two feet.

At this time, the Newfoundland sealing fleet had already slipped out of the hands of the outporters. The sailing vessels were larger than they had been in the early years of the century and most were owned by St. John's merchants. Impressed by the strength of the steam whalers, they bought two in 1863. The steamers took only 4,300 seals that year, but more were bought and in 1873, 22 steam ships returned with more than 300,000 sculps. These were the famous "wooden walls" of Newfoundland, the sealing fleet that became an island legend. Nearly all the wooden ships eventually died in the ice, but the mystique of sealing did not die with them. Although today's sealing ships are modern steel vessels, and primarily Norwegian-owned, Newfoundlanders continue to imbue sealing with a rather misplaced aura of adventure and romance.

A seal pup at sunset.

Like medieval men rallying to the call of a crusade, the outporters left their humble homes in February and headed for St. John's, a straggling army of thousands trudging on foot across the wintry island. In St. John's all was bustle and activity. In the harbor, the gloomy, dark-timbered, battle-scarred ships were readied for another fight with the ice. In town, the captains, men of island-wide fame, handed out berth tickets with the air of feudal lords bestowing favors. Each man signed for his "crop," essential sealing implements, worth at most $9, for which $12 would be deducted at the end of the journey from his meager share of the hunt.

It did happen, though rarely, that after six weeks or more of incredibly hard work and suffering, a sealer's share would only equal the value of his crop, and he would wander homewards, penniless.

The fleet left early in March. The ships, designed for 40 or 50 extremely crowded whalers, now carried 150 to 200 sealers. Most slept in the hold, a filthy, fetid, gloomy hellhole, curling up anywhere they could find space. They had no beds, no bunks, no blankets. For work on ice and in frequent freezing storms, the men arrived in scanty clothing. Many wore jackets made of old bags "ragged and extensively bepatched," George Allan England observed in 1922, and then exlaimed: "Poverty! Lord, what poverty!"

Until about 1900, the St. John's merchants who made fortunes out of sealing, added to their profits by the simple expedient of not feeding the sealers. Until they reached the seals, the men subsisted on hardtack and tea, after that on seal meat, often eaten raw, especially the hearts. Later, grudgingly, warm meals were supplied, 'fish and brewis' (hardtack boiled with cod), and 'duff,' hefty dumplings, of India rubber consistency when warm and aptly known as 'cannonballs' when cold, and an endless supply of potent tea, sparingly sweetened with molasses. The men ate where they slept, in the grimy cavern of the ship, in the pallid light of blackened lanterns, heated by ancient bogeys that scattered ashes and belched soot and smoke.

It was not all hardship. The men were bound together by a rough and honest camaraderie. On rare free nights, they sang ancient chanteys. Many could recite poems by the hour. Above all, they talked of "swilin'," of other trips and other hunts. They were the legionnaires of the ice, reliving old battles and hardships, revelling in tales of toil and danger. And all looked forward eagerly to the "tumult and fury of the hunt," England noted, because "not for mere gain do men endure such miseries as the hunt entails." It was their war: the ice their enemy, the seals their victims. It had the spice of gambling. A ship might be crushed by ice, a crew lost, or it might return 'log-loaded' in less than two weeks. In 1901, the *Southern Cross* sailed straight into the heart of the 'main patch' and was back in St. John's, loaded to capacity, in 11 days. In 1914, the *Southern Cross* again loaded with pelts, this time taken in the Gulf, got caught in a storm on the way home. She never arrived. Lost with her were 173 men. "The sea is made of mothers' tears," is a Newfoundland saying.

In the early years of the 19th century, the sealers, hunting with open boats or small shallops, left Newfoundland in late March or early April, in part to avoid a blow from "Patrick's brush," as they called the vicious equinoctial gales frequent around Saint Patrick's Day. As the ships employed in the hunt became bigger, and rivalry fiercer, the hunt started earlier. A few ships left already in February, some in the hope of a quick kill and a full load, a hurried trip to St. John's to unload their cargo, and out again for a second and, perhaps, even a third trip in the same season. In 1880, the steamer *Walrus* (lost in the ice in 1908), damaged early in March, returned for repairs to St. John's. While the rest of the fleet searched the remote pack, the *Walrus* found seals on ice fields close to the coast, took a full load, returned to the ice for a second load, and took a third within sight of St. John's. As catches declined, from an average of 400,000 seals per year between 1820 and 1860, to 300,000 per year between 1860 and 1900, a statute was passed in 1895 forbidding second trips, "to preserve the seal herds from extinction."

Finally, March 15 was set as the opening date of the seal hunt and most ships left St. John's around March 10. Thus the peak of the hunt coincided with the time the pups were fattest, their sculps yielded the most oil, and the hunt the greatest possible profit. One or two ships usually went "to the back" of the island, to hunt seals in the Gulf of St. Lawrence. The others headed "to the front," traveling north, when ice permitted, on the "inside cut," open water between Newfoundland's east coast and the pack ice.

All hands were worried then, for where in all this vastness were the seals? Some years, the Front ice might cover an area of more than 150,000 square miles. Somewhere in this immensity of current-carried, wind-driven ice spread over a region three times the size of England, the seals were hauling out to whelp. Many a ship had sailed into the ice, got stuck for weeks and never saw a seal. To come home "clean" meant hardship and disgrace.

Dark, grimy ships belching black smoke, squeezed and pressed their way through the infinite world of dazzling white. Their captains keenly watched each other's progress. Some captains, famous for their ability to find the seals, were dogged by other ships and tried by feint and subterfuge to shed their unwanted company. Joy was to be first into the "young fat." Joy, too, was to leave a rival behind, hopelessly trapped in ice, far from the seals. Like elite troops, the men took pride in their courage, pride in the skill and cunning and ruthlessness of their captains, pride in their hardy, battered ships. And, like the arctic whalers, they paid dearly for their daring. Of 194 whaling vessels working out of Hull between 1772 and 1852, 80 were lost in the ice. Of 50 steam sealers working out of St. John's between 1863 and 1900, 41 did not return.

The owners did not worry. A "full" ship yielded handsome profits. Insurance paid for a lost ship. The men, who so willingly and courageously risked their lives, counted for little on the balance sheets. They were "sacrificed to greed for gold," wrote William Coaker, founder and editor of the newspaper "The Fishermen's Advocate" in 1914. That year 253 sealers died. To their families the companies paid nothing. Asked why a radio had been removed when its presence might have saved the lives of 77 sealers who died in terrible agony on the ice because their captain assumed they were on another ship, a company representative explained that the radio had not paid for itself. "The safety of the crew was not thought of at all," he admitted to the commission inquiring into the tragedy. All in all, from the owners' point of view it had not been such a bad year. True, 253 men had died, but others were keen to take their place. And the ships had returned with 234,000 seal pelts.

On the ships steaming through the immense ice fields, anticipation and tension mounted until, one day, from the lookout high at the masthead came the jubilant cry: "Whitecoats!" Then all rushed to the railing and stared with eager, avid eyes across the ice. As the ship passed a solitary pup near the edge of the herd, a man, with cat-like agility, slipped overboard, jumped from floe to floe, clubbed and skinned the pup, and rushed after the moving ship, while his comrades yelled and cheered. Back aboard with the sculp, he presented the pup's sliced-off little tail ceremoniously to the captain with the wish for "fifty thousand more!" If they had reached the 'main patch,' the ice would be dappled with seals as far as the eye could see, and in the leads and pools seals were cavorting and diving. Entranced, George Allan England watched them. "They flung up sheaves of foam that flashed in scattered rays of sunshine... swift, joyous forms that plunged, rolled, and dived in dashing froth; Nature's supreme last word in vital force and loveliness and grace." And then the killing started. It was, the sealers said, "the number one excitement of the year."

Above left:
Near a pressure ridge, a female seal in
threat posture.

Above right:
A sealing ship works its way through the
ice on the "Front" to reach the seal herds.

Chapter seven
"Death Is No Rare Visitor."

They were the army of the ice, disciplined and tough and eager, fiercely loyal to their captains and their calling. They slaughtered seals from dawn to dark, worked half the night to stow the load aboard, and were abroad again at dawn. They roamed the ice, five thousand men from many ships, dark shapes upon the blinding white. They jumped from floe to floe and killed and hauled and slaved and where they passed, the ice turned red. They were the men of iron and of blood.

The sailing fleet of old made little or no headway in heavy ice. Captains skirted the pack, searched for leads, advanced when the ice went slack and were stuck when it tightened. The men worked near the ships, killing seals in the vicinity, then struggled back, hauling the heavy sculps.

The steamers were more mobile. The men were organized in "watches," each group led by a master watch, a veteran sealer. As the steamer approached the edge of a breeding patch, a group went overboard, the ship barely slowing, and the men jumped over the breaking, buckling floes to get clear of the ship's destructive path. Watch after watch went over the side, scattered on the ice, and advanced on a broad though rather irregular front, killing all the seals in their path. Most females escaped, abandoning their pups. Those that remained were slain together with their young.

The men wore 'skinnywoppers,' Eskimo-style sealskin boots, their soles studded with sparables to provide a grip on the slippery ice. The more provident carried 'nunch bags' with provisions, usually just a handful of hardtack, and some spare clothing. Each sealer carried a gaff, its shaft six to seven feet long, to kill the seals, to use as an ice pole when vaulting from floe to floe, and in emergencies, to hook a comrade out of the sea. And all carried tow ropes to haul the heavy sculps.

When winter came, a favorite sport of outport youth was 'copying' from floe to floe across the bays and coves that faced their homes. They learned to judge the strength of ice, hopped flea-quick over tiny floes that held them for a second and then sank, and after frequent dunkings grew wary of 'pummy,' the ground-up ice between the pans, that often looked so solid but was gruel-soft.

"Death Is No Rare Visitor."

An old-time sealing ship in the "Front" ice.

*They were the army of the ice,
disciplined and tough and eager.*

On long winter evenings, the boys listened with fascination as their elders spun tales of the great hunt, told of seals that covered the ice for miles, told of hunger and hardship and hope, of awesome dangers and miraculous rescues, of captains who, their men averred, could neither read nor write but who could smell the seals a hundred miles away. Raised on such tales of daring and adventure, it was small wonder that most outport boys dreamt of going to the ice. To be a sealer was a mark of manhood. Many went on their first voyage when they were but 15 or 16 years old and after that, come spring, the lure of going on another hunt was irresistible. Old Abram Kean, the famous "commodore" of the sealing fleet, went to the ice for 67 years.

Their early training on the floes stood the sealers in good stead as they advanced across the treacherous ice. About them, the air was filled with the wailing of the pups. "The crying of a herd of whitecoats is something not easily forgotten," wrote the Newfoundland journalist-politician William Coaker, who went along on a sealing trip in 1914. "It is a pitiable cry, and it seems hard to slaughter those innocents." But, like hunters everywhere, and men in slaughterhouses, the sealers could ill afford to feel compassion for their prey.

A sealer whacked the pup across the head with the heavy gaff smashing its thin-boned skull, turned the twitching corpse belly-up, slit it from chin to scutters (hind flippers) with a smooth stroke of his long, razor-sharp knife, and sliced the sculp, the pelt plus underlying blubber, from the body, together with at least one flipper, for seal flippers were (and are) a Newfoundlander's favorite food. Most sealers could sculp a pup neatly, without nicking the skin or leaving a sliver of meat on the fat, in a minute, and some could do it in forty seconds. Captain Robert Bartlett reached the main patch one year in late afternoon, and in the few hours before dark his men killed, sculped and 'panned' 8,000 seals.

Land-based sealers, caught in a snowstorm, haul a boat-load of sculps across the ice of the Gulf of St. Lawrence.

The panning was the hardest part. The sculps taken in one area had to be dragged and piled onto a central, sturdy pan, well marked by an ownership flag on a tall pole. Bent double the men hauled their heavy 'tow,' four or five sculps, each weighing close to 40 pounds, across the slippery, hummocky ice, or from floe to floe, when the pack was slack. Crimson trails criss-crossed the ice, "man's mark and sign and signal in the North," George Allan England said.

England admired the sealers: "A braver, more heroic breed of men never lived," but the occasional, and casual, cruelty of the hunt sickened him: "Some of the seals, appallingly vital creatures, are not at all dead as they are hauled in on gaffs. They writhe, fling, struggle. Here comes a baby with a gaff point jammed through its jaw. Here a mother seal, bleeding in slow and thick runnels. Both at ship's side are rolled belly up and slit."

The men advanced across the ice. Their ship steamed after them to pick up the panned pelts. Clanking and groaning it winched them aboard, load after load, and flopped them down in heaps upon the blood and grease-coated deck. The carcasses were left upon the shimmering ice, food for the pure-white, high arctic ivory gulls, lured this far south by promise of a yearly feast, and later, as the floes disintegrated, for sharks and crabs. "The waste in our sealing industry is appalling," wrote Sir Wilfred Grenfell in 1934. George Allan England, too, felt outraged: "Millions of pounds... are every year thrown away... In this hungry world, the sheer flinging away of these immense masses of edible meat is downright criminal."

Sculps, too, were frequently lost. Most captains, once they reached the seals, were anxious to clean up, to forestall rivals who might muscle in. They killed and panned, shifted their men, and killed and panned some more, and kept this up for days, until the ice was bare of life, retraced their course and picked up the panned pelts. If all went well, this was the fastest way to fill a ship and foil the rivals. In 1910, Captain Abram Kean commanding the *Florizel* was home in 17 days with a full ship. But often weather intervened. Spring gales shrieked across the ice, the floes shifted, the panned pelts went adrift, never to be retrieved. One spring, sealing in the Gulf, the men of Captain Bartlett's ship killed and sculped 52,000 seals. Half they recovered, the rest were lost.

Not all the missing sculps were always truly lost. Most sealing captains were deeply pious, men of the sternest rectitude: some did not drink, some frowned on swearing. But when it came to unattended sculps, left by a rival on a pan, temptation frequently won over righteousness and the sculps ended up in their hold. With nearly all of them, sealing was an obsession, and every captain's dream was to be 'high-liner' of the year, to sail home to acclaim with the largest load of sculps.

A sealer on the Gulf ice tows sculps towards a central pile.

As night came to the ice, each steamer searched for its scattered flock. Bone-weary, 'muckered' men trudged toward their ship, received a hasty supper, usually boiled seal or duff, and went to work again. They winched more sculps aboard, and chunks of ice. They stowed the sculps below, each separated from the next by a layer of chopped ice. They built pounds, so that their slippery cargo would not shift. They hauled coal to the engine room, and dumped ash overboard. And when the hold was filled with sculps, they ripped out bunks and piled them into cabins and on deck. The little *Neptune* once came home, well-nigh awash, with 32,000 sculps below and on deck, and towed another 6,000 behind her on a long rope. Near midnight, the work was usually done, the men curled up wherever there was space, slept soundly for four hours, received their tea and hardtack and went to the ice again.

The ships plowed on, shuddering and groaning, their steel-sheathed bows bucking the ice. High in the masthead barrel the 'scunner' scanned the vastness of the ice, looking for seals to kill, and leads and lanes to reach them. As days turned into weeks, men and ships became coated with grime and grease and gore. The stench of rancid oil pervaded the ships. Decks, steps and corridors were darkened by coal dust and ash, slimy with grease. As it became warmer, the smell of putrid gurry, oil and blood, rose from the bilges. The drinking water, melted snow or ice in iron tanks, turned red with rust and blood, and when sculps were loaded, rivulets of blood and oil ran from the scuppers. The sealers did not mind. It was the smell and signal of success. It was their toast before they left St. John's: "Bloody decks and many of them!"

Nor were they overly concerned with the fire hazard aboard their ships. From stem to stern and mast to bilges the wooden ships were soaked in oil, as inflammable as gasoline. Stored somewhat haphazardly in each ship were kegs and cans of powder and boxes of dynamite, used to blast the ice when ships were jammed. In this setting, inviting disaster, men casually smoked, dropped glowing butts or knocked out pipes, lanterns smouldered, and ancient cracked bogeys sputtered sparks. When a ship did catch fire, she went up like a gas-soaked torch. In 1931, the 500-ton *Viking*, a former whaling ship built in Norway in 1881, hit a large pan at a slant, heeled over sharply, and a bogey tore loose scattering flaming coals. The powder caught, exploded and within moments the ship was a blazing pyre. Twenty-nine men died, and many more were horribly burned and maimed.

Before, early in this century, doctors, or at least men with some notion of medicine, were employed on sealing ships, the captains usually dealt with accidents, using carpenter's tools and limited medical supplies. A man whose arm got mangled in a winch, received a stiff shot of rum, his arm was cut off with a saw, the bone filed down, the arteries were tied off with catgut, smaller veins cauterized with silver nitrate, and the stump bandaged. The patient received another glass of rum and that was it. It speaks for the sealers' hardihood and health that they usually survived such "operations."

"These men think often of death," George Allan England said of the sealers, for "death is no rare visitor." And death rarely came quickly or gently. To most it came as the finale to excruciating suffering that preceded it. How many died is not known. It is perhaps indicative of the Newfoundland seal hunt and its priorities that we have superlative statistics on the number of seal pelts brought to St. John's each year, from 1800 to the present day — 118,080 in 1810, 685,530 in 1844, 183,689 in 1936 — but no one bothered to keep count of the men who died in pursuit of all this wealth. "More than thousand," say most reports on sealing. The thousands more who returned crippled were not even mentioned. From the statistical and financial point of view, it was the seals that mattered, not the men. Only the most spectacular disasters were recorded in some detail.

A list of sealing ships and their fate reads like a dirge of death: "Crushed by ice"; "Abandoned in sinking condition"; "Lost on rocks in snowstorm"; "Lost with all hands." Sometimes a ship returned, but many of its men did not. In 1854, 73 sealers were caught on a floe in a raging gale. As the men died, the survivors used their bodies to build a breakwater to protect them from the icy spray lashing across the floe. When the whaler *Orion* found them, three men, near death, lay huddled behind a wall of 70 corpses. In 1898, the men of the *Greenland* (lost in 1907) worked far from their ship when a storm struck the ice. Forty-eight froze to death. In 1914, 120 men of the *Newfoundland*, most of them poorly dressed, were on the ice for 56 hours in a fierce storm and bitter cold. Seventy-seven died.

Above, left and right:
In long straggling file, sealers haul sculps across the ice and "pan" their catch on a solid floe to be picked up by their ship.

One spring, high winds and ice forced many of the ships to seek refuge in Battle Harbour on the Labrador coast. All made it just before dark, except the *Huntsman*. She ran upon a reef that ripped her bottom out. Next day, the people of Battle Harbour spotted something at Fish Rock, the highest point of the reef. It was Solomon French, the lone survivor of the *Huntsman*. All night he had clung to the small, slippery rock, half in water, his body battered by the waves, both legs smashed by the pounding ice. He did survive, his legs were set, and he went back to sealing.

"The men love the adventure, but get little monetary return," Sir Wilfred Grenfell noted in 1934. But there was always that beacon of hope. In 1910, the *Florizel* under Captain Abram Kean, returned with 46,069 sculps worth $90,000. Her 203 sealers received one third of this, $148 for each man, a princely sum. This was, of course, exceptional, but it became a magic figure in every sealer's dream. The average share was about $35. Even this pittance they needed desperately. One day, with the simple pathos of the very poor, an old work-worn sealer, twelve of whose fourteen children had died young, confided in George Allan England that the worst had come to pass. His wife, he said, insisted on having a set of false teeth and with those, he feared "her'll eat a wonnerful lot more, an' I doubts if I can reach to feedin' she."

"Sealing is a hard life. It is more dangerous than exploring the Arctic; there's no question about it," wrote Captain Robert (Bob) Bartlett, of sealing and of arctic fame. He was captain of the *Roosevelt* on two of Peary's expeditions and in 1909 he went with Peary to the pole, breaking trail, while Peary followed, husbanding his strength. At 133 miles from the goal, Bartlett, at Peary's orders turned back. In 1913 he commanded the *Karluk*, Vilhjalmur Stefansson's expedition ship. She broke up in 1914 near Wrangel Island. Bartlett sledged to Siberia, hundred miles away, and made his way from there to Alaska to get help. Later he went back to sealing, for the Bartletts had been sealers for more than a century. His father, William Bartlett was a sealing captain for 42 years.

They were a special breed, these sealing captains, the Windsors, Blackwoods, Barbours, and the Keans, who went 'swiling,' man and boy, through every generation. Hard-driving men, they were obsessed with sealing, with hauling in the biggest load. Their men revered them and served them with nearly feudal fealty, due to their status and their aura of success. And tough and successful they were. In 1934, Captain Abram Kean at 79 returned to St. John's with his millionth seal. For this he received the Order of the British Empire.

If the captains were famous, many of their ships achieved even greater fame. In 1884, the *Bear* and the *Thetis* reached northern Ellesmere Island to save the survivors of the Greeley expedition. The *Bear*, subsequently rounded Cape Horn and became Alaska's most famous ship. It was the *Bear* which took the first reindeer from Siberia to Alaska in 1892. The 200-ton, 40-year-old sealer *Nimrod* (Antarctica's great Nimrod glacier is named after it) was Ernest Shackleton's expedition ship, and Robert Scott went on his fateful voyage to Antarctica in the most famous sealing ship of all, the *Terra Nova*. Launched in Dundee in 1884, she was a carvel-built, bark-rigged three-masted steamer of 400 tons. Scott sailed in her in 1910, through heavy antarctic ice where, he wrote, "no other ship... would have come through so well... As she bumped the floes with mighty shocks, crushing and grinding a way through some, twisting and turning to avoid others, she seemed, like a living thing fighting a great fight." Three years later the *Terra Nova* returned with the survivors of the expedition and the diaries of its gallant leader. The next year she was back sealing. George Allan England sailed on her to the "Front ice" in 1922, a "scarred, time-bitten old ship... dark, dingy, coal-dusty and dirtier than anything I have ever seen... dreary and repellent."

In 1906, a rival made of steel joined the hard-worked, ice-gouged 'wooden walls.' The *Adventure*, 800 tons, was strongly built, with thick steel plating, extra-heavy beams and rocker bow. Instead of bucking ice, she rode up upon the floes and crushed them with her weight. Others soon followed, bigger, more powerful: the *Nascopie*, 1,000 tons; the *Florizel*, 2,000 tons; the *Stephano*, 2,100 tons; sealers in spring, passenger ships or freighters the rest of the year. The wooden ships struggled on, grimy, neglected, their ranks reduced by loss in ice and storm year after year. In 1942, only three remained, the *Eagle*, *Ranger* and *Terra Nova*. That year the *Ranger* sank, veteran of the ice for three-quarters of a century. In 1943, the *Terra Nova* sank while carrying supplies for the armed forces. And in the early 1950s, the ancient *Eagle*, last of her race, was towed to sea and set afire, a fitting Viking funeral for an ancient, gallant ship.

Ships changed, but the traditional rhythm of the hunt remained. For two or three weeks after the official start of the hunt on March 15, the men killed pups, and any females remaining near them. Then the surviving pups shed their natal fur and, clad in short-haired, grey, dark-dappled coats, took to the sea, and the sealers looked for other prey, for "hoods" and adult "harps."

The hooded seals are larger than the harp seals, less abundant and more dispersed. Widely scattered, they lie on the ice in family groups: the massive, powerful "dog hood," weighing as much as 800 pounds, the female, weighing about 400 pounds, and her pup, its lovely fur a slatey blue above, changing to creamy white below. Unlike the meek and timid harps, the hooded seals stand their ground and, when approached, attack. It helped them little. The sealers shot the adults and clubbed the pups.

On right:
A mother knows her own offspring. The one
in the background will be cuffed if it
comes too close.

They also shot the adult harp seals, lying in thousands upon the ice during this period when they were beginning their annual moult. As April advanced, the ice receded, and the sealers followed the retreating ice fields and the seals towards the north. This was a very different kind of hunt from the one earlier when the pups were killed. Now the men roamed the ice in teams of two, a 'gunner' and his 'dog,' his helper carrying the heavy bag with ammunition.

It was a risky race across the floes, rising and falling on the swell. They jumped from floe to floe, crouched low to hide behind some hummocks, stalked and shot, sculped the seal, and on they moved, while far behind them their ship zigzagged through the ice to pick up pelts. They kept it up, day after day, harrying the retreating herds, hauling in a few dozen seals on bad days, a few hundred on good ones. Some captains, loath to leave as long as there were any seals left to kill, pursued the herds well into May. But by then their cargo began to ooze oil in such amounts, that the additional sculps barely made up for the loss of oil draining away into the bilges.

It was a wasteful hunt. Old Captain Kean reckoned that in the hunt of adult harps, for every seal shot and retrieved, another 20 were killed and lost.

The seal hunt, wrote Sir Wilfred Grenfell "is a question of hustle and rapid returns" and in 1934 he warned: "There is no question that the seals are diminishing in numbers." Statistics bore him out. The great hunts of the 19th century, when 400 ships with 10,000 men returned with half a million seals were over. In the latter part of the 19th century the average kill declined to 300,000 per year. There still were years, when ice and weather conditions were exceptionally favorable, that the sealers "wiped clean" the ice: in 1902 they returned with 527,686 sculps. But the trend was downward and after World War I, rare was the year that the kill surpassed 200,000.

In part, this was due to lack of ships and lack of financial incentive. In 1916, the *Stephano* was torpedoed and sank off Nantucket Island. In 1918, the *Florizel* struck Horn Head Point, on Newfoundland's east coast, in a storm at night and 94 of her passengers and crew died, among them Captain Joe Kean, son of Abram Kean. The price of seal products dropped. In 1933, they were considerably below World War I levels. In 1906, 25 steamers with 4,061 men went to the ice, and returned with 341,836 sculps. In 1936, only eight steamers left St. John's with 1,460 men, and they took 183,689 seals. And these were mostly super-annuated vessels, the last of the 'wooden walls,' grime-coated ships near death.

On the whole, it was a period of decline, with fewer ships, lower profits, greater risks and poorer pay. The sealers suffered most. There was a feeble effort to curtail the hunt. In 1922, a government inspector went along on sealing ships, in theory to enforce a few quite gentle regulations. In practice he rarely intervened. The one aboard George Allan England's ships "must have been a total paralytic, blind, deaf, and otherwise disabled," for he was rarely seen and never heard. The captains still were kings, but even they began to worry. If large and efficient ships guided by spotter planes (introduced in 1921) reached the main breeding patch with unfailing certainty each year, "that would be the beginning of the end," Captain Abram Kean wrote in 1936.

In 1942, three of the ancient wooden ships went out, and two returned. Then sealing ceased. The ships and men were needed for another kind of war. After the war, the price of pelts was high. The hunt was resumed with redoubled vigor: with fast steel ships guided by spotter planes, with helicopters that brought sealers to the ice and hauled back the pelts. Increasingly, Norwegian sealers and Norwegian-owned ships dominated the hunt. The kill soon soared to a quarter million and more each year. In 1964, 85 per cent of all the pups born on the Front were killed, 170,000 of them. Plus 60,000 adult seals. In one decade, from 1950 until 1960, half of the herd was destroyed.

"Observers and writers are not wanted by the seal hunters" George Allan England had noted in 1922. In the 1960s, a superabundance of both descended upon the sealers. The hunt had become big news. It could not fail. The seal pups, white and cute and cuddly, were innocence incarnate. Protection groups took up their cause and demanded a halt to the hunt.

Now a host of regulations governs the hunt. Quotas are set. The pro- and anti-sealing factions bombard each other and the public with a welter of conflicting claims and figures. The hunt goes on; so do the campaigns to halt the hunt; each side certain in the righteousness of its cause.

Far on the ice, of Gulf and Front, the harp seals that remain, perhaps a million now, pursue the ancient rhythm of their life, oblivious to man's concern.

Death has passed it: on the ice a pup plays with its flipper.

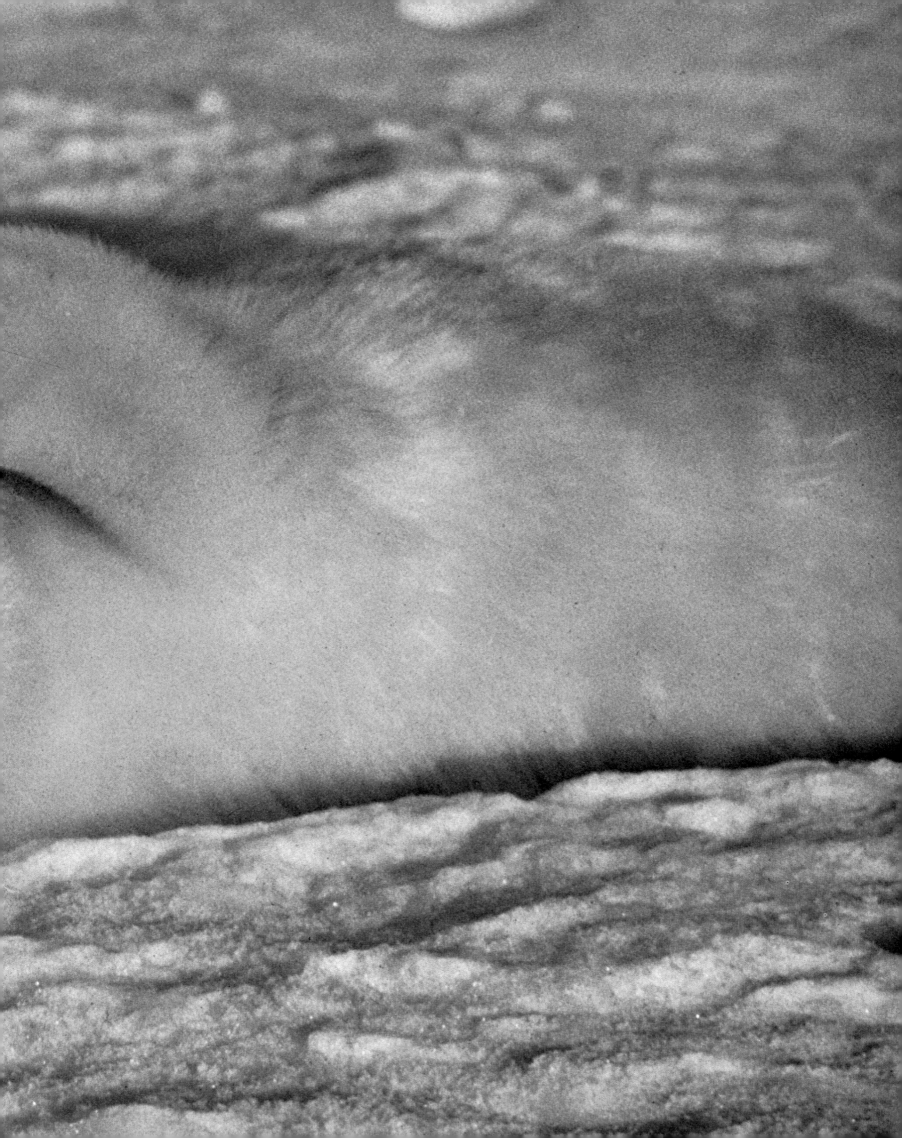

Chapter eight
And Life Goes On.

Death has walked across the ice and passed. The harp seal pups, now two weeks old, begin to moult their silky, woolly natal fur. They are immensely fat. The puny pups that weighed just 18 pounds at birth, have since more than tripled their weight and nearly doubled their girth. They look like furry, flippered blimps.

To grow fat and expand, that is the essence of their young lives, for soon they will be on their own. During their first two weeks they slept, expending a minimum of energy, awoke to drink their mothers' fat-rich milk, and slept again, gaining weight at an average rate of three-and-a-half pounds each day. The pure-white luster of their natal fur is dimmed; the short, dark-grey hairs of the new coat beneath shine through and give it a gentle ashen cast.

The baby wool begins to shed, on head and back and flippers first. The wind carries wisps of the gossamer fleece across snow and ice. The pups look patchy and scruffy. 'Ragged-jackets,' Newfoundland sealers call the moulting pups. Their hair follicles are changing and they itch. But the pups are too tubby and their flippers too short to alleviate itching by scratching. So they twist and turn and churn upon the snow and ice, trying to ease themselves.

The female seals are restless. For a few days after the birth of the pups most remained near them, nursing them whenever they awoke, hungry and whimpering. Then the females began to leave from time to time, to swim beneath the ice or in the nearby pools, and after a while they rejoined their pups. Now most females are near estrus; subtle hormonal changes influence their behavior. The strong bond of devotion to their pups begins to weaken.

Near a canted slab of ice a female lies beside her pup. Her fur is a silvery greyish-brown, her head jet-black. Across her flanks and back stretch the distinctive black saddle-shaped patches to which the harp seals owe their name. 'Saddlebacks,' they are also called. They mark her as a mature animal. But no external signs indicate her exact age. Only her teeth show it, for their dentine and cementum are laid down in annual layers, like growth rings of a tree. It is this which enables biologists to determine the age of dead seals with great accuracy.

Above left:
After two to three weeks, the female
harp seals leave the ice and the pups.

On right:
Relatively small at birth, pups gain
weight at an incredible rate.

The shortening days of fall and the increasing cold begin to drive the harp seals south. To linger can be fatal. Ice crystals form in the cooling sea and coalesce in the calmer bays and fiords into a cover of young ice, thin, tough and razor-sharp. Occasionally some seals tarry too long in a food-rich fiord. Ice forms across its entrance and locks them in. As the barrier grows thicker and each day larger in extent, and their area of open water contracts, the seals must haul out and hump laboriously across the ice towards the distant open sea. 'Crawlers' they call them on the coast of Labrador and they are easy prey for polar bears and man.

The seals swim south, quite leisurely, twenty to thirty miles each day, ahead of the advancing ice. In early October, the first pods pass Cape Chidley, the gaunt, grey, lichen-spattered northernmost tip of Labrador. By mid-December they are off Belle Isle. Here the herds divide. Those of the Front continue south and east, to spend winter on the Grand Banks. Those of the Gulf turn west and swim through Belle Isle Strait into the Gulf of St. Lawrence. The juveniles and many bedlamers lag far behind. They have no pressing date upon the ice in March. Most are still along the ice-free Greenland coast and may dawdle there well into January. Bringing up the rear of the adult migration are the older males. 'Pat Jones' they call them on the coast of Labrador, a corruption of the French 'pattes jaunes,' the yellow-flippers.

Among the seals swimming into the Gulf is the young female that was wooed so ardently, and won, upon the ice last March, northwest of Brion Island. In April, after moulting, she weighed a scant 250 pounds. Since then, during summer and fall's long feast, she has gained more than 70 pounds, and is well padded with blubber three inches thick.

In mid-February, beneath a wan and wintry sun, she seeks the ice fields in the Gulf. In early March she hauls out on a floe, not far from where she was born. The night is still and clear and cold. A film of ice spreads over pools and leads and breaks with a sibilant, rustling sound in the wavelets created by surfacing seals.

The voices of the seals drift across the ice, the snarl of angry females, the plaintive mewing of newborn pups. The night begins to change. A faint rose suffuses the eastern sky and traces the edges of wispy indigo clouds. The soft glow of morning spreads over the ice. The young female groans and shifts her heavy, gravid body. Her womb contracts, the pup slides out upon the ice, a steaming, gleaming parcel of life. The rays of the rising sun slant across the ice and tint the floes in nacre and gold. The female nuzzles her pup and inhales deeply its smell that marks it as her very own. The pup stirs and begins to cry, the feeble, urgent call of a new life.

Bibliography

Backer, Ole Friele. *Seal Hunting Off Jan Mayen.* National Geographic Magazine, Vol. 93, No. 1 Washington, 1948.

Backhouse, K.M. *Seals.* Arthur Barker Ltd. London, 1969.

Bartlett, Robert A. *The Sealing Saga Of Newfoundland.* National Geographic Magazine, Vol. 56, No. 1. Washington, 1929.

Beck, Brian. *Seal Net Fisheries Along The North Shore Of The St. Lawrence River.* Trade News. Department Of Fisheries of Canada. Aug.-Sept. 1965. Ottawa, 1965.

Biggar, Henry P. *Samuel de Champlain*, 6 Vols. Champlain Society. Toronto, 1922-1936.

Biggar, Henry P. *The Voyages Of Jacques Cartier.* Ottawa, 1924.

Boilieu, Lambert de. *Recollections Of Labrador Life.* Saunders, Otley & Co. London 1861. Reprinted by the Ryerson Press, Toronto, 1969.

Brown, Cassie and Horwood, Harold. *Death On The Ice.* Doubleday Canada Ltd. Toronto, 1972.

Brown, Cassie. *A Winter's Tale.* Doubleday Canada Ltd. Toronto, 1976.

Bruemmer, Fred. *Encounters With Arctic Animals.* McGraw-Hill Ryerson Ltd. Toronto, 1972.

Bruemmer, Fred. *The Arctic.* Optimum Publishing Co. Montreal, 1974.

Burton, Maurice. *The Sixth Sense Of Animals.* J.M. Dent & Sons Ltd. London, 1973.

Callanan, J.T. *The Newfoundland Seal Hunt.* Published in *The Book Of Newfoundland*, J.R. Smallwood, editor. Newfoundland Book Publishers Ltd. St. John's, 1937.

Chafe, L.G. et al. *Chafe's Sealing Book, A History Of The Newfoundland Seal Fishery From The Earliest Available Records Down To And Including The Voyage Of 1923.* The Trade Printers And Publishers Ltd., 1923.

Chiasson, Anselme. *Les Légendes Des Iles De La Madeleine.* Editions Des Aboiteaux. Moncton, 1969.

Cromie, William J. and the Editors of Reader's Digest. *Secrets Of The Sea.* The Reader's Digest Association. Pleasantville, New York, 1971.

Cumming, W.P. et al. *The Discovery Of North America.* McClelland and Stewart Ltd. Toronto, 1971.

Dagg, Anne I. *Canadian Wildlife And Man.* McClelland and Stewart Ltd. Toronto, 1974.

Daniel, Hawthorne and Minot, Francis. *The Inexhaustible Sea.* Dodd, Mead & Co. New York, 1958.

Davies, Brian. *Savage Luxury.* Souvenir Press. London, 1970.

Dembeck, Hermann. *Animals And Men.* The Natural History Press. Garden City, New York, 1965.

England, George Allan. *Vikings Of The Ice.* 1924. Reprinted as *The Greatest Hunt In The World.* Tundra Books. Montreal, 1969.

Fogarty, James R. *The Seal Skinner's Union.* Published in *The Book Of Newfoundland*, J.R. Smallwood, editor. Newfoundland Book Publishers Ltd. St. John's, 1937.

Freuchen, Peter and Salomonsen, Finn. *The Arctic Year.* Putnam. New York, 1958.

Greendale, R.G. and Brousseau-Greendale, C. *Observations Of Marine Mammals At Cape Hay, Bylot Island During The Summer Of 1976.* Environment Canada. Fisheries And Marine Service Technical Report No. 680. Ottawa, 1976.

Green, William H. *The Wooden Walls Among The Ice Floes*. Hutchinson & Co. (Publishers) Ltd. London, 1933.

Grenfell, Wilfred. *The Romance Of Labrador*. The MacMillan Company. New York, 1934.

Harrison, R.J. and King, Judith, E. *Marine Mammals*. Huchison University Library. London, 1965.

Harrison, R.J. et al, editors. *The Behavior And Physiology Of Pinnipeds*. Appleton-Century-Crofts, Meredith Corporation. New York, 1968.

Harrison, R.J., editor. *Functional Anatomy Of Marine Mammals*. Academic Press, London & New York, 1972.

Hatton, Joseph and Harvey, M. *Newfoundland*. Doyle and Whittle. Boston, 1883.

Iversen, Thor. *Drift-Ice And Sealing*. Manuscript report. Oslo, 1926.

Jangaard, P.M. *The Capelin*. Department Of The Environment. Fisheries And Marine Service. Bulletin 186. Ottawa, 1974.

Kean, Abram. *Commentary On The Seal Hunt*. Published in *The Book Of Newfoundland*, J.R. Smallwood, editor. Newfoundland Book Publishers Ltd. St. John's, 1937.

Keating, Bern. *The Grand Banks*. Rand McNally & Co. New York, 1968.

King, Judith E. *Seals Of The World*. Trustees Of The British Museum (Natural History). London, 1964.

Lavigne, David M. *Life Or Death For The Harp Seal*. National Geographic Magazine. Vol. 149, No. 1. Washington, 1976.

Mansfield, A.W. *Seals Of Arctic And Eastern Canada*. Fisheries Research Board Of Canada. Bulletin No. 137. Ottawa, 1967.

Mansfield, A.W. *Population Dynamics And Exploitation Of Some Arctic Seals*. Antarctic Ecology, Vol. I. 1970.

Maxwell, Gavin. *Seals Of The World*. Constable & Company Ltd. London, 1967.

Mercer, M.C. *The Seal Hunt*. Information Branch, Fisheries And Marine Service. Department Of Fisheries And The Environment. Ottawa, 1977.

Morison, Samuel Eliot. *The European Discovery Of America*. Oxford University Press. New York, 1971.

Mowat, Farley and Blackwood, David. *Wake Of The Great Sealers*. McClelland and Stewart Ltd. Toronto, 1973.

Moyles, R.G. *Complaints Is Many And Various But The Odd Divil Likes It (Nineteenth Century Views Of Newfoundland)*. Peter Martin Associates. Toronto, 1975.

Neary, Peter and O'Flaherty, Patrick, editors. *By Great Waters (A Newfoundland And Labrador Anthology)*. University Of Toronto Press. Toronto, 1974.

Peattie, Donald C., editor. *Audubon's America*. Houghton Mifflin Company. Boston, 1940.

Rumily, Robert. *Les Iles De La Madeleine*. Les Editions Chanteclerc. Montreal, 1951.

Scheffer, Victor B. *Seals, Sea Lions And Walruses*. Stanford University Press, 1958.

Scheffer, Victor B. *The Year Of The Seal*. Charles Scribner's Sons. New York, 1970.

Sergeant, D.E. *Exploitation And Conservation Of Harp And Hood Seals*. The Polar Record, Vol. 12, No. 80. 1964.

Sergeant, D.E. *Migrations Of Harp Seals Pagophilus Groenlandicus (Erxleben) In The Northwest Atlantic*. Journal Of The Fisheries Research Board Of Canada. 22:433-64. Ottawa, 1965.

Sergeant, D.E. *Reproductive Rates Of Harp Seals*. Journal Of The Fisheries Research Board Of Canada. 23(5). Ottawa, 1966.

Sergeant, D.E. *Migration And Orientation In Harp Seals*. Proceedings Of The Seventh Annual Conference On Biological Sonar And Diving Mammals. Stanford Research Institute. Menlo Park, California, 1970.

Sergeant, D.E. *Feeding, Growth, And Productivity Of Northwest Atlantic Harp Seals (Pagophilus groenlandicus)*. Journal Of The Fisheries Research Board Of Canada, 30(17). Ottawa, 1973.

Sergeant, D.E. *Estimating Numbers Of Harp Seals*. Rapp. P.-v. Réun. Cons. Int. Explor. Mer. 169:274-280. 1975.

Sergeant, D.E. *History And Present Status Of Populations Of Harp And Hooded Seals*. Biological Conservation, 10(2). 1976.

Sivertsen, Erling. *On The Biology Of The Harp Seal*. Det Norske Videnskaps-Akademi I Oslo, Nr. 26. Oslo, 1941.

Stuart, Frank. *The Seal's World*. McGraw-Hill Book Company Inc. New York, 1954.

Terhune, David. *The Harp Seal*. Burns & MacEachern Ltd. Toronto, 1973.

Vibe, Christian. *The Marine Mammals And The Marine Fauna In The Thule District (Northwest Greenland) With Observations On Ice Conditions in 1939-41*. Meddelelser Om Grønland, C.A. Reitzels Forlag. Copenhagen, 1950.

Vibe, Christian. *Arctic Animals In Relation To Climatic Fluctuations*. C.A. Reitzels Forlag. Copenhagen, 1967.

Printed in Canada

Text: Optima Medium
Paper: Optimum Dull, 80 lb.

12-2977

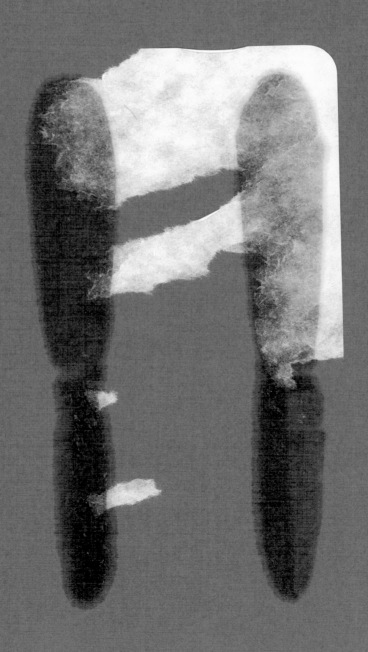